DANIEL

DANIEL

INSIGHT ON THE LIFE AND DREAMS OF THE PROPHET FROM BABYLON

PAUL YONGGI CHO

Creation House
Lake Mary, Florida

Copyright © 1990 by Paul Yonggi Cho
All rights reserved
Printed in the United States of America
Library of Congress Catalog Card Number: 90-55271
International Standard Book Number: 0-88419-302-0

Creation House
Strang Communications Company
600 Rinehart Road
Lake Mary, FL 32746
(407) 333-0600

Contents

Preface

The book of Daniel is the Old Testament's parallel to the New Testament's book of Revelation. Daniel himself didn't fully understand the contents of his prophecy about the last days, but he faithfully wrote what he had received from God.

As early as 600 B.C. Daniel wrote a book of remarkably accurate predictions about things that would happen in the last days and provided an outline of human history as well. In fact, the prophecies in the book of Daniel about the centuries just after Daniel's time came true in history so accurately that modern critics who disbelieve that genuine prophecy can take place have asserted that all the fulfilled predictions had to have been composed *after* the events they describe, no earlier than the Maccabean period (second century B.C.). But through the guidance of the Holy Spirit we are assured that such assumptions about the impossibility of prophecy are wrong.

We who live in this apocalyptic age should well know how to interpret the signs of the times. It has been my strong desire to write an exposition of the book of Daniel ever since I wrote one about the book of Revelation. I thank God for the fulfillment of this dream now, and I feel as if a heavy debt has been at least partially paid.

This exposition of the book of Daniel has been written for lay readers in a popular style like a sermon, instead of in a scholarly style for specialists, just as my study of the book of Revelation was written.

My sincere wish is that this book will become a guide that will enlighten the wisdom of the people who live in this apocalyptic age so that they may serve the Lord more fervently.

The first edition of this title was first published in the Korean language in August 1976.

Paul Yonggi Cho

1

The Character of Daniel

Daniel, the Captive (1:1-2)

In the third year of the reign of Jehoiakim king of Judah, Nebuchadnezzar king of Babylon came to Jerusalem and besieged it. And the Lord gave Jehoiakim king of Judah into his hand, along with some of the vessels of the house of God; and he brought them to the land of Shinar, to the house of his god, and he brought the vessels into the treasury of his god.

When the northern kingdom of Judah fell to Babylon's King Nebuchadnezzar in 606 B.C., young Daniel was among the Jews who were taken captive and carried away to Babylon. But he was promoted to a high government position in Babylon and also in Persia, where he was later carried as a captive when that empire succeeded Babylon. As an administrator in the courts of these kingdoms, Daniel gained wide respect both from his fellow Jewish exiles and from pagans. At the same time, he remained as a faithful servant of God for his whole lifetime.

Daniel was a prominent political figure of the day serving seven kings successively in the Babylonian court: Nabopolassar (625-604 B.C.), Nebuchadnezzar (606-561 B.C.), Amel-Marduk (561-560 B.C.), Neriglissar (559-556 B.C.), Labishi-Marduk, (556 B.C.), Nabonidas (555-536 B.C.). After the downfall of Babylon, he then served Darius the Mede and Cyrus in the Persian court.

Babylon, where Daniel spent most of his life, was the foremost city in the world of his day, and its glory as the capital of a powerful empire continued for more than seven decades. According to archaeological findings today, it was an enormous city. Babylon was shaped like a square, with the perimeter of its four sides totaling fifty-six miles, with the length of each side being fourteen miles. The city wall, made of brick, was as high as three hundred feet in some places and went down thirty-three feet beneath the surface of the earth so that enemies could not tunnel under it. It was eighty feet thick.

This city was famous for its fabulous buildings. It boasted the great temple of Marduk, the Babylonian god, and the luxurious palaces of Nebuchadnezzar. In addition, the famed Hanging Gardens, one of the so-called seven wonders of the ancient world, hung in the air artificially from terraced slopes.

Nevertheless, just as Isaiah prophesied, Babylon was overthrown like Sodom and Gomorrah, and now nothing remains but its ruins (see Is. 13:19-22). Great Babylon disappeared with the magnificence of its kings, like passing clouds. Yet the revelation of God, about whom Daniel wrote, remained alive and is still held in our hands. That revelation is the book of Daniel which we will study.

Let's look first at how the Israelites were conquered by the Babylonians and carried away as captives.

[handwritten top margin: Law = Sabbatical year / Ground rested every 7th yr. / Lev 25:1-7]

The State of Israel

Israel is God's chosen people. God called Israel and loved her like the apple of His eye. She is the posterity of Abraham, Isaac and Jacob, who received the promise from God.

Yet God's chosen people were taken captive and carried away to Babylon, the sinful land which did not know the true God but served pagan gods. The treasure of the house of the Lord was taken as spoils, and the land that flowed with milk and honey was turned into a desolate place. Why was Israel forsaken and smitten by God in this way?

First, Israel was forsaken because the people forsook the law and the promise of God. God gave the promise as well as the law to the Israelites through Moses, but they ignored the law of God and lived as they pleased.

The Bible often compares God to a husband and the Israelites to his wife. The wife was wanton and left her husband like an adulterous woman. She declared that she was independent from her husband, and she disregarded the law and the promise.

[handwritten margin: Israel = wife of God (Church His Bride)]

What if your own spouse, whom you had trusted and thought to be a vital part of your life, had become treacherous in that way? You would probably burn with jealousy and seek to help your spouse correct his or her ways. This is simply the nature of things. In such a situation, what spouse in the world would remain a mere spectator?

How much more then would the righteous God, our Father, do? So God, who had been waiting for Israel to repent and to return to Himself, finally used Babylon, a Gentile nation, to discipline Israel.

[handwritten margin: 1.) turned from God]

Second, Israel not only had broken the law of God; it had violated the Sabbath and the sabbatical year. God had commanded Israel to work for six days of the week and rest on the seventh day, for it was holy to Him (see Ex. 20:8-11). God

[handwritten margin: 2.) Broke a law - Sabbath / Sabbath year / Hebrew servant released in 7th yr.]

11

had also commanded that the Israelites should set free a Hebrew servant in the seventh year when the six years' service was finished, no matter what the circumstances under which he had been sold (see Ex. 21:2). Concerning the land, God had commanded that for six years they should sow the land and gather in its fruit, but the seventh year they should let it rest (see Lev. 25:1-7).

Israel, however, did not keep these commands of God. So God clearly foretold that He would make Israel desolate as punishment for their wickedness (see Lev. 26:14-46; Jer. 34:12-22).

Third, the nation worshipped idols. The first of God's commandments said, "You shall have no other gods before Me" (Ex. 20:3). But Israel committed spiritual adultery by serving the Baals and Asherahs, the Canaanite gods and goddesses, while they lived in the land of Canaan. How could God leave them unpunished?

Fourth, idolatrous nations inevitably degenerate into moral corruption. The moment they leave the righteous God, the power of God which makes them live according to conscience and the standards of morality leaves them. This happened to Israel as well.

When Israel thus left God and became adulterous and degenerate, God decided to destroy the nation. God had warned His people repeatedly through His prophets, such as Isaiah and Jeremiah. Nevertheless, Israel did not turn back from its wickedness. So God finally delivered Israel into the hand of Nebuchadnezzar of Babylon.

Babylon had to have God's permission to do this. Unless God permits it, human armies cannot smite as they wish. The beginning and the end of world history today are still in the hand of God.

During the Korean War, for example, God delivered our republic into the hand of the communists. Like Israel, Korea, in the providence of God, had been called to preach the gospel to the nations of the world. Yet like Israel, our nation forgot the command and covenant of God and walked the path of corruption and immorality. So God delivered us into the hand of the communists. Through these circumstances God made us undergo repentance and an awakening which brought forth the growth of the Korean church.

Nevertheless, if our nation forsakes the commandment and covenant of God and departs from His holiness, no one can say with certainty that God will not strike this land again. On the contrary, if we realize the burden God has given to us and serve Him well, obeying all of His commandments, we will receive wonderful blessings from God, blessings of heaven and blessings of earth.

The Youth Who Were Elevated to High Positions (1:3-7)

Then the king ordered Ashpenaz, the chief of his officials, to bring in some of the sons of Israel, including some of the royal family and of the nobles, youths in whom was no defect, who were good-looking, showing intelligence in every branch of wisdom, endowed with understanding, and discerning knowledge, and who had ability for serving in the king's court; and he ordered him to teach them the literature and language of the Chaldeans. And the king appointed for them a daily ration from the king's choice food and from the wine which he drank, and appointed that they should be educated three years, at the end of which they were to enter the king's personal service. Now among them from the sons of Judah were Daniel, Hananiah, Mishael and Azariah.

Then the commander of the officials assigned new names to them; and to Daniel he assigned the name Belteshazzar, to Hananiah Shadrach, to Mishael Meshach, and to Azariah Abed-nego.

Because God delivered Jerusalem into the hand of Nebuchadnezzar, he easily captured the city and took some of the articles from the temple, carrying them to the temple of his own god for the treasure house there. Besides this, he carried away most of the inhabitants of Jerusalem to Babylon as captives. Out of the captives carried to Babylon, Nebuchadnezzar picked some young men who were handsome and intelligent to serve in his court.

From this we can conclude that Nebuchadnezzar was a wise king. When he conquered a country, he not only captured its material treasures like gold and silver, but also its human treasures. He made it a policy to take intelligent people from the country and carry them to his own land, training them for the development of his own kingdom.

Among the young men chosen out of the royal family and nobility of Israel were Daniel, Hananiah, Mishael and Azariah. For three years they were taught the language and the literature of the Chaldeans in the school of the palace. Ashpenaz, chief of court officials, gave new names to these young men after the names of Babylonian gods. Because they were captives and were specially favored by their conqueror, they could not refuse the pagan names given to them.

But Daniel made up his mind that he would not defile himself with the king's choice food or with the wine which he drank; so he sought permission from the commander of the officials that he might not defile himself (1:8).

14

In this passage we notice how firm was the faith of Daniel. From ancient times the Jews were famous for loyalty to their religion. This may be one of the main reasons why they have kept their integrity as a people in spite of two thousand years as a wandering people all over the world.

Look at the unfaltering faith of Daniel. He was a young man specially chosen from among many youths to be admitted to the royal school of Babylon. Others might have taken pride in that. Nevertheless, he clung to the faith of his forefathers. He made up his mind not to defile himself like the heathen Babylonians.

The food was royal food, appointed by Nebuchadnezzar himself who ruled the world of his day. So it is not difficult to imagine the sumptuousness of his table. Yet Daniel determined not to eat this kind of food because of God's laws.

Heathens of Daniel's day had no restrictions on what foods were allowed to them. In Leviticus 11, however, the Mosaic law prohibited the Jews from eating certain kinds of food. For instance, the Jews could not eat insects; animals such as pigs, camels and rabbits; marine animals without fins or scales; or birds which belonged to the eagle or owl families. So Daniel was afraid that he might unknowingly violate the commandment of God if he ate the royal food of the Babylonian court.

Did not want to violate the law unknowingly.

Another reason Daniel refused the royal food was that it had first been offered to idols before it was eaten. It was the custom of that day for all the meat and wine served to the king to be first offered to the Babylonian god Merodach. Accordingly, if Daniel ate the food, it meant that he acknowledged idols. So he refused.

This problem of food offered to idols—which occurred in the New Testament church as well (see 1 Cor. 8:7)—may not be common in modern America. But in some countries today, such as Korea, it can still be an issue. Daniel provides us with an example. The Bible says that we must not eat food we think has been sacrificed to an idol or offered in a service of exorcism, as is traditional in the Korean culture. We may eat food as long as we do not know its source, but if we eat such food after we learn its source, we will fall into the temptation of Satan and find ourselves in agony because we feel guilty about it.

The Young Men Are Rewarded (1:9-16)

Now God granted Daniel favor and compassion in the sight of the commander of the officials, and the commander of the officials said to Daniel, "I am afraid of my lord the king, who has appointed your food and your drink; for why should he see your faces looking more haggard than the youths who are your own age? Then you would make me forfeit my head to the king." But Daniel said to the overseer whom the commander of the officials had appointed over Daniel, Hananiah, Mishael and Azariah, "Please test your servants for ten days, and let us be given some vegetables to eat and water to drink. Then let our appearance be observed in your presence, and the appearance of the youths who are eating the king's choice food; and deal with your servants according to what you see."

So he listened to them in this matter and tested them for ten days. And at the end of ten days their appearance seemed better and they were fatter than all the youths who had been eating the king's choice food. So the overseer continued to withhold their choice food and the wine they were to drink, and kept giving them vegetables.

Because Daniel resolved not to defile himself with the royal food and wine sacrificed to idols, in the integrity of his faith he asked the chief official, "Give us nothing but vegetables to eat and water to drink."

His supervisor was afraid. On one hand, the official might have considered the request profitable because he could keep the royal food and drink assigned to Daniel and his three friends as his own. On the other hand, the request seemed to be dangerous because if the king saw the youths looking haggard, the king would have his head. Accordingly, the official did not accept Daniel's request.

Nevertheless, Daniel persisted and suggested a test of diet that would allow the official to determine whether the young men's health would suffer. Though they ate nothing but vegetables and drank nothing but water, at the end of ten days they looked healthier and better nourished than any of the young men who ate the royal food. So the chief official granted with pleasure Daniel's request to eat vegetables only.

We can learn from this episode that if we resolve to maintain the integrity of our faith God will always take care of the problems that may arise from our resolution.

The Servants God Trained (1:17-21)

And as for these four youths, God gave them knowledge and intelligence in every branch of literature and wisdom; Daniel even understood all kinds of visions and dreams. Then at the end of the days which the king had specified for presenting them, the commander of the officials presented them before Nebuchadnezzar. And the king talked with them, and out of them all not one was found like Daniel, Hananiah, Mishael and Azariah; so they entered the king's personal service. And as for every

matter of wisdom and understanding about which the
king consulted them, he found them ten times better than
all the magicians and conjurers who were in all his
realm. And Daniel continued until the first year of Cyrus
the king.

When Daniel and his three friends did not defile themselves but kept the command of God, despite the hardships of captivity in Babylon, God loved them and took care of them.

The Bible says in Deuteronomy (28:1-14) that a number of blessings will come upon a nation if that nation keeps the commands and law of God, neither turning aside to the right nor left, nor following other gods and serving them. That nation will be set high above all nations on the earth. The fruit of the womb and kneading trough among its people will be blessed. Though its enemies come from one direction, they will flee in seven. God will send rain on the land in season and will make the land produce bountiful crops. The people will lend to many nations but will borrow from none. God will make the nation the head, not the tail.

The God who gave us such a promise is the faithful creator of the whole universe. When He opens the door, no one can shut it, and when He shuts the door, no one can open it.

God saw integrity in the faith of Daniel who trusted in Him. So He gave Daniel knowledge and understanding in all kinds of literature and learning, making him wiser than anyone else in the land. God does the same thing today. So when your children want to violate the Lord's day with the excuse that they must study, teach them this lesson. Make them first serve the Lord and then study in the remaining hours. The Lord will honor their integrity and bless their study.

Meanwhile, as their parents, pray for your children every morning and night, laying your hands on them to bless them.

All wisdom and understanding are blessings granted by God. If God lets His Spirit dwell upon a person so that he or she may receive wisdom and understanding, that person can achieve great learning which no one in the world can challenge.

The same is true with businesspeople—serving the Lord must come first. Too often we see Christian businesspeople who are so absorbed in their business that they neglect their duty as Christians. They neither attend worship services nor give God their tithes, which is His due.

They forget God. Peace and joy disappear from their heart. And since all the blessings of wealth come from God, is it possible for them to keep their wealth safely? Of course not. What good is it to accumulate money with so much trouble?

When we put our trust in the treasure of the earth, that treasure will disappear in just a brief time. But if we put our trust in God as our first and last, relying only upon Him and allowing Him to govern our lives, God will abundantly pour out His blessings upon us. We will receive the spiritual blessings of peace of mind and a joyful heart as well as the material blessing of earthly gain. I pray in the name of the Lord Jesus Christ that all of you may possess the kind of faith with integrity that Daniel had.

After the young men's three-year training period in the court school was completed, Nebuchadnezzar put them to a test. He was amazed to find that Daniel and his three friends were ten times better in wisdom and understanding than all the magicians and enchanters in Babylon. In addition, Daniel could understand visions and dreams of all kinds. So Nebuchadnezzar had them serve in the council of his court.

We should remember that God set these young men in the highest positions in Babylon when they served Him first and kept His commands, even though they were prisoners from the small foreign country of Judah. So wonderful is God's providence!

2

Nebuchadnezzar's Forgotten Dream

The King's Demand (2:1-6)

Now in the second year of the reign of Nebuchadnezzar, Nebuchadnezzar had dreams; and his spirit was troubled and his sleep left him. Then the king gave orders to call in the magicians, the conjurers, the sorcerers and the Chaldeans, to tell the king his dreams. So they came in and stood before the king. And the king said to them, "I had a dream, and my spirit is anxious to understand the dream."

Then the Chaldeans spoke to the king in Aramaic: "O king, live forever! Tell the dream to your servants, and we will declare the interpretation." The king answered and said to the Chaldeans, "The command from me is firm: if you do not make known to me the dream and its interpretation, you will be torn limb from limb, and your houses will be made a rubbish heap. But if you declare the dream and its interpretation, you will receive from me gifts and a reward and great honor; therefore declare to me the dream and its interpretation.''

The second chapter of Daniel deals with Nebuchadnezzar's forgotten dream. The king had a dream which depicted coming events in world history. God gave Nebuchadnezzar this dream 2,600 years ago to show the outline of world history from his time to the time of Jesus' coming to this earth.

Even though the king was a daring man with a heroic temper, he couldn't sleep because the dream was so fearful and awesome. So the king wanted to know the interpretation of the dream.

According to the Scriptures, Nebuchadnezzar must have been a wise king, for when he summoned the magicians and enchanters of his palace to tell him the interpretation of the dream, he didn't tell them what he had dreamed. He knew that when most people hear someone's dream they are usually able to provide a plausible interpretation of it. So how much less difficult would it be for the Babylonian magicians and enchanters who were specially trained to interpret!

They answered a second time and said, ''Let the king tell the dream to his servants, and we will declare the interpretation.'' The king answered and said, ''I know for certain that you are bargaining for time, inasmuch as you have seen that the command from me is firm, that if you do not make the dream known to me, there is only one decree for you. For you have agreed together to speak lying and corrupt words before me until the situation is changed; therefore tell me the dream, that I may know that you can declare to me its interpretation.'' The Chaldeans answered the king and said, ''There is not a man on earth who could declare the matter for the king, inasmuch as no great king or ruler

*has ever asked anything like this of any magician, con-
jurer or Chaldean. Moreover, the thing which the king
demands is difficult, and there is no one else who could
declare it to the king except gods, whose dwelling place
is not with mortal flesh." Because of this the king
became indignant and very furious, and gave orders to
destroy all the wise men of Babylon. So the decree went
forth that the wise men should be slain; and they looked
for Daniel and his friends to kill them (2:7-13).*

When the king demanded that they tell the interpretation of
the dream without hearing what he had dreamed, they protested.
But the king refused to change his mind and insisted that they
should produce the dream and its interpretation together. Only
then would he know for certain that they could interpret the
dream correctly.

Being pressed, the magicians slyly shuffled the responsibil-
ity to the gods. This made the king so furious that he ordered
the execution of all the wise men of Babylon and the destruction of their houses. The commander of the king's guard went
out with soldiers to execute his orders, and the situation became
grave.

The Bold Faith of Daniel (2:14-16)

*Then Daniel replied with discretion and discernment
to Arioch, the captain of the king's bodyguard, who
had gone forth to slay the wise men of Babylon; he
answered and said to Arioch, the king's commander,
"For what reason is the decree from the king so
urgent?" Then Arioch informed Daniel about the matter.
So Daniel went in and requested of the king that he
would give him time, in order that he might declare the*

interpretation to the king.

The fate of Daniel and his three friends, Shadrach, Meshach and Abednego, hung by a thread. But notice here the boldness of those who trust in God. The people were frightened out of their senses by the king's command to execute all the magicians and enchanters of Babylon. But Daniel, who trusted in the eternal God, was unperturbed. Instead he simply asked the king for some time to seek the Lord for the interpretation.

Daniel's response should remind us that we can trust God in difficult situations without panicking. In ordinary times there may seem to be little difference between the life of a Christian and that of a non-Christian. Once adversity comes, however, a great difference is manifested. Those who do not trust in Jesus Christ are easily frustrated and tend to complain. They grow uneasy and try to escape the circumstances, as the pagan magicians did. On the other hand, Christians can overcome crisis and hardship like Daniel, relying upon God with bold faith.

The Revelation of God (2:17-19)

Then Daniel went to his house and informed his friends, Hananiah, Mishael and Azariah, about the matter, in order that they might request compassion from the God of heaven concerning this mystery, so that Daniel and his friends might not be destroyed with the rest of the wise men of Babylon. Then the mystery was revealed to Daniel in a night vision. Then Daniel blessed the God of heaven....

Being faced with the harsh and hasty decree of the king, Daniel called his three friends to him, and they held a prayer meeting.

Notice here that the prayer of two people is better than the prayer of one person, and the prayer of more than two is even better. Daniel was a man who knew the power of corporate prayer. The urgency of the king's decree might have sent him to a mountain to pray alone. But instead he called his friends, and they prayed together.

This principle, which I call the "law of companions in prayer," is still true today, especially for our families. The prayer of a couple is more desirable than the prayer of only one person, and the prayer of the whole family is even better— especially when we are praying for revelation from God. If those who have fervent faith pray together according to this law, God will answer that prayer more quickly.

After the four friends prayed to God, during the night God revealed Nebuchadnezzar's dream to Daniel in a vision. I believe that this means Daniel dreamed the same dream Nebuchadnezzar had dreamed. Accordingly, he could know everything in Nebuchadnezzar's dream.

When Daniel awakened the next morning, he praised God:

Daniel answered and said,
"Let the name of God be blessed forever and ever,
For wisdom and power belong to Him.
And it is He who changes the times and the epochs;
He removes kings and establishes kings;
He gives wisdom to wise men,
And knowledge to men of understanding.
It is He who reveals the profound and hidden things;
He knows what is in the darkness,
And the light dwells with Him.
To Thee, O God of my fathers, I give thanks and praise,
For Thou hast given me wisdom and power;
Even now Thou hast made known to me what we
*   requested of Thee,*

For Thou hast made known to us the king's matter''
(2:20-23).

We can see in Daniel's response to God's revelation an example to follow: He had a heart of true gratitude.

Daniel Tells the King About God (2:24-30)

Therefore, Daniel went in to Arioch, whom the king had appointed to destroy the wise men of Babylon; he went and spoke to him as follows: "Do not destroy the wise men of Babylon! Take me into the king's presence, and I will declare the interpretation to the king."

Then Arioch hurriedly brought Daniel into the king's presence and spoke to him as follows: "I have found a man among the exiles from Judah who can make the interpretation known to the king!" The king answered and said to Daniel, whose name was Belteshazzar, "Are you able to make known to me the dream which I have seen and its interpretation?" Daniel answered before the king and said, "As for the mystery about which the king has inquired, neither wise men, conjurers, magicians, nor diviners are able to declare it to the king. However, there is a God in heaven who reveals mysteries, and He has made known to King Nebuchadnezzar what will take place in the latter days. This was your dream and the visions in your mind while on your bed. As for you, O king, while on your bed your thoughts turned to what would take place in the future; and He who reveals mysteries has made known to you what will take place. But as for me, this mystery has not been revealed to me for any wisdom residing in me more than in any other living man, but for the purpose of making the interpretation known to the king, and that you may understand the thoughts of your mind.

Finally Daniel was brought into the presence of the king to tell him both the mysterious dream and its interpretation. Yet notice that Daniel did not come to the king simply to tell the dream and its interpretation. He stood before the king with a determination to make the most of this opportunity to be a witness of the true God before the king.

The same should be true for us. Whenever we have a conversation with someone who is not a Christian, we should make it our goal to preach Jesus Christ through that conversation so that the person may accept Him as Lord and Savior.

The Contents of Nebuchadnezzar's Dream (2:31-43)

"You, O king, were looking and behold, there was a single great statue; that statue, which was large and of extraordinary splendor, was standing in front of you, and its appearance was awesome. The head of that statue was made of fine gold, its breast and its arms of silver, its belly and its thighs of bronze, its legs of iron, its feet partly of iron and partly of clay. You continued looking until a stone was cut out without hands, and it struck the statue on its feet of iron and clay, and crushed them. Then the iron, the clay, the bronze, the silver and the gold were crushed all at the same time, and became like chaff from the summer threshing floors; and the wind carried them away so that not a trace of them was found. But the stone that struck the statue became a great mountain and filled the whole earth.

This was the dream; now we shall tell its interpretation before the king" (vv. 31-36).

Surely the king was astounded by Daniel's accuracy. So Daniel no doubt had the king's attention as he went on to give the interpretation of each element of the dream.

> *"You, O king, are the king of kings, to whom the God of heaven has given the kingdom, the power, the strength, and the glory; and wherever the sons of men dwell, or the beasts of the field, or the birds of the sky, He has given them into your hand and has caused you to rule over them all. You are the head of gold"* (vv. 37,38).

Daniel's interpretation that the golden head in the dream was Nebuchadnezzar himself must have been a great shock to the king. Until then he had thought he had become a king by his own merit and by the blessing of his god, Merodach. So he could only be astonished when he heard that Daniel's God had made him a king. Yet he could not refute what Daniel had said, because Daniel had revealed every secret of his heart which he had kept to himself.

> *"And after you there will arise another kingdom inferior to you, then another third kingdom of bronze, which will rule over all the earth"* (v. 39).

The breast of silver will be dealt with more specifically in chapter 7, but we should note briefly here that it refers to the coalition kingdom of Media and Persia, which conquered Babylon at the time of Belshazzar. The breast of silver has two arms, representing the two members of the coalition. These two kingdoms alternately ruled what had been the whole region of Babylonia.

The belly of brass follows the breast of silver. This refers to the Greek age of Alexander the Great, who conquered the Medo-Persian kingdom. Babylon and Medo-Persia, which had ruled before the Greek empire, were Asian kingdoms. Alexander the Great, however, arose and brought under his control Macedonia in Europe, Iran and Syria in western Asia and even Egypt in Africa. He built the Greek empire by uniting the East and the West.

Thus the brass which formed the belly extended to the thighs and was divided into two parts because Alexander the Great built a kingdom extending both to the East and the West and breaking the coalition of the Medo-Persian kingdom. One leg refers to the West and the other to the East.

> *"Then there will be a fourth kingdom as strong as iron; inasmuch as iron crushes and shatters all things, so, like iron that breaks in pieces, it will crush and break all these in pieces. And in that you saw the feet and toes, partly of potter's clay and partly of iron, it will be a divided kingdom; but it will have in it the toughness of iron, inasmuch as you saw the iron mixed with common clay. And as the toes of the feet were partly of iron and partly of pottery, so some of the kingdom will be strong and part of it will be brittle. And in that you saw the iron mixed with common clay, they will combine with one another in the seed of men; but they will not adhere to one another, even as iron does not combine with pottery"* (vv. 40-43).

Next come the legs of iron. After the fall of Alexander the Great, the kingdom he had built was divided into four parts by the four generals who had been his staff officers. They lasted for only a short period and were conquered by Rome, which arose at that time. Because Rome established a kingdom, the territory which extended to the east and the west is represented by the legs of iron.

DANIEL

Daniel points out in particular that the kingdom of iron would be strong and would subdue the world. The Roman empire was in fact the strongest and the most terrible empire in history. Its army broke other nations to pieces, just like the legs of iron.

In addition, part of the feet and toes were iron and part were clay. This signified that the kingdom would be divided. Part of it would be strong and part of it would be weak at the same time.

The Age of the Toes

I believe that the age represented by the toes of mixed iron and clay refers to the present age. If that is the case, you may well ask, then what about the two thousand years that elapsed between the period of the iron legs—the time of the Roman empire, which saw the first coming of Jesus—and the present age?

This is the period I call the gospel age. And I believe that God did not disclose this gospel age of Jesus Christ when He gave revelation to the Jewish prophets because these two thousand years are the age in which God calls His bride, the church, according to His special providence. This is why in Daniel's prophecy the description of the Roman empire is immediately followed by a description of the establishment of Christ's kingdom on earth—that is, Christ's coming to this earth.

The ten toes of both feet thus show that ten nations will be somehow united in the former territory of the eastern and western parts of the Roman empire. Yet this unity will be difficult to maintain because some of the member countries will be ruled by imperialist or authoritarian regimes, while others will be countries ruled by democratic governments. Such a unity—involving nations governed by different political philosophies—can only be incomplete.

You may ask whether such a period will actually come in history. If Daniel's book is an accurate and sure prophecy, then this age is without a doubt the very age of the toes. And if these toes—the ten nations—are on the way toward unity, we are sure to be approaching the end of the world.

What is happening then around us? The movement to unify Europe, in the former territory of the Roman empire, has been briskly underway since 1958. The headquarters of the European Economic Community (EEC) was established that year in Brussels, Belgium. Its task has been to unify Europe economically, and now plans are being laid for political unity as well.

Presently we cannot predict with certainty when this political unity will be accomplished. But one thing is certain. Unless Europe is unified, it cannot survive. Its leaders know that it cannot compete with the superpowers of the world in its present fragmented condition. Consequently, by the divine providence which works in history and in nature, Europe is slowly marching toward unity, and that unity will first be accomplished economically and politically.

At a certain day and hour in our lifetime, I believe we will hear through the news media that the unity of ten nations of Europe has finally been achieved. All over Europe they will have elected their representatives to the European Parliament, and the European Parliament will have elected the president of Europe. Then the drama of the end times will speed up dramatically.

According to my understanding of other passages from the Bible, especially in Revelation, in that period the antichrist will arise and enter into a seven-year treaty of friendship with Israel. Then the great tribulation will start, and around that time the church will be taken up into heaven. The church will be swept up by the wind of the Holy Spirit, and eternal destruction and tribulation will come upon the people remaining on this earth.

The Stone Cut Without Hands (2:44-45)

"And in the days of those kings the God of heaven will set up a kingdom which will never be destroyed, and that kingdom will not be left for another people; it will crush and put an end to all these kingdoms, but it will itself endure forever. Inasmuch as you saw that a stone was cut out of the mountain without hands and that it crushed the iron, the bronze, the clay, the silver, and the gold, the great God has made known to the king what will take place in the future; so the dream is true, and its interpretation is trustworthy."

When Europe has been unified, a stone which is not cut by human hands will strike the image—that is, will bring down the pride of human empire—thereby bringing an end to history. In this time of the toes, we are told, God will set up a kingdom that will never be destroyed, nor will it be left to another people besides God's people. It will crush all human kingdoms and bring them to an end, but it will itself endure forever.

This kingdom is the eternal kingdom of Christ, and the stone which was cut out in heaven refers to Jesus Himself. The Bible says, "The stone which the builders rejected, this became the chief corner stone; this came about from the Lord, and it is marvelous in our eyes" (Matt. 21:42).

Jesus is the very stone that God uses to accomplish His purposes. Like the prophecy recorded in Revelation 19, this prophecy tells of things that will happen in the future when Jesus descends to this world riding on a white horse to bring an end to the war of Armageddon. He will come down with His saints who participate in the marriage supper. With them He will destroy all the armies of the earth and will throw the beast—the anti-Christ—into the fire of sulphur, casting into hell all the people who have the mark of the beast. After all these things He will set up the millennial kingdom.

These things will come true quickly. I believe it may happen before our generation passes. If it does, Paul tells us, then at that time

> ...the Lord Himself will descend from heaven with a shout, with the voice of the archangel, and with the trumpet of God; and the dead in Christ shall rise first. Then we who are alive and remain shall be caught up together with them in the clouds to meet the Lord in the air (1 Thess. 4:16,17).

Such a prophecy is being fulfilled before our very eyes in current events. Daniel saw it all through a vision 2,600 years ago. We, however, know about it through historical events which have actually happened. So in that regard we now live in the happiest of all ages.

The Lesson Concerning Human History

The picture of human history Daniel saw showed the deterioration of human civilization. Nebuchadnezzar's kingdom was gold, but the following kingdoms were increasingly inferior: silver, brass, iron and finally clay.

Today many people say that, with the improvement of education, human civilization will progress. Actually, however, it grows worse as time goes on, and its character will deteriorate into "clay." This is the reality Daniel saw through the revelation of God twenty-six centuries ago.

On the other hand, however, the imagery in Daniel suggests

that the world will become stronger militarily. In specific gravity, gold is 19; silver is 11; brass is 8.5; and iron is 7.8. In degree of hardness, however, silver is superior to gold; brass is superior to silver; and iron is much superior to brass. This implies that the more human civilization develops, the more dreadful weapons and military power it will possess.

Furthermore, with regard to political forms, the imagery suggests that each kingdom's political power will be weaker. The kingdom of gold, for example, represents a government with supreme power. Nebuchadnezzar completely organized the entire domain of Babylon and held the fate of all its subjects in one hand. But Medo-Persia, though it ruled a larger territory than Babylon, was weaker in political power. Such a phenomenon became more conspicuous in the Greek kingdom and in the succeeding Roman empire. The Roman dominions were eventually split in half, the east and the west, under the reign of Valentinian I in A.D. 364. Then Rome finally fell to the invading barbarians. In the period of the toes, the iron and clay are mixed together, implying that this period will be characterized by weaker political power rather than totalitarianism.

Nebuchadnezzar Surrenders to God (2:46-49)

Then King Nebuchadnezzar fell on his face and did homage to Daniel, and gave orders to present to him an offering and fragrant incense. The king answered Daniel and said, "Surely your God is a God of gods and a Lord of kings and a revealer of mysteries, since you have been able to reveal this mystery." Then the king promoted Daniel and gave him many great gifts, and he made him ruler over the whole province of Babylon and chief prefect over all the wise men of Babylon. And Daniel made request of the king, and he appointed Shadrach, Meshach and Abed-nego over the administration of the province of Babylon, while Daniel was at the king's court.

When Daniel revealed the vision he had seen in his dream and interpreted it, Nebuchadnezzar was so impressed that he fell upon his face and worshipped Daniel. The king of a great kingdom actually came down from his throne and worshipped an exile! Since he thought Daniel was a messenger of God, he commanded that offerings and incense be presented to the young man.

Of course, this behavior was not actually directed toward Daniel himself. Nebuchadnezzar sacrificed offerings, burned incense and bowed himself down to the God of Daniel who gave him wisdom and understanding. He offered worship to God in the same way he normally worshipped his own god, Merodach.

We must not misunderstand here and think that Daniel received worship as if he were God. He knew that the object of the king's worship was actually the Lord Himself rather than Daniel.

Afterward, Nebuchadnezzar set Daniel in a high position and made him ruler over the entire province of Babylon, placing him in charge of all its wise men. Moreover, at Daniel's request, the king appointed Shadrach, Meshach and Abednego, who had prayed with Daniel, to be administrators over the province of Babylon.

Notice closely how much Daniel's circumstances had changed. He began as an exile attending a three-year course at the court school. He almost lost his life during the disturbance caused by Nebuchadnezzar's dream. But when he gathered together his friends and prayed to God, he received the divine revelation by which all the hardships turned into blessings.

This is the difference between those who believe in God and those who do not. When unbelievers are not able to solve the difficulty that comes to them, they are torn to death by the adversity. On the other hand, believers of God counter this difficulty with the concerted prayer of fellow Christians. Consequently, the difficulty is finally overcome, and they receive the miracle of God's turning everything into good in the end. In this way believers receive the blessings promised in Deuteronomy: They become not the tail, but the head; they do not decline, but rise; they do not borrow, but lend.

For that reason, we who believe in God give thanks in all the circumstances of our lives. For when good things come to us, we are grateful, and even though bad things come to us, we are sure they will turn into good things.

3

The Fiery Furnace

Nebuchadnezzar the king made an image of gold, the height of which was sixty cubits and its width six cubits; he set it up on the plain of Dura in the province of Babylon. Then Nebuchadnezzar the king sent word to assemble the satraps, the prefects and the governors, the counselors, the treasurers, the judges, the magistrates and all the rulers of the provinces to come to the dedication of the image that Nebuchadnezzar the king had set up. Then the satraps, the prefects and the governors, the counselors, the treasurers, the judges, the magistrates and all the rulers of the provinces were assembled for the dedication of the image that Nebuchadnezzar the king had set up; and they stood before the image that Nebuchadnezzar had set up (vv. 1-3).

In the eighteenth year of the reign of King Nebuchadnezzar, and twenty years after Daniel had become an exile, the king

37

set up a ninety-foot golden image to be worshipped. I believe that the image must have been the very same image Nebuchadnezzar saw in his dream. He was probably so puffed up by Daniel's interpretation that the golden head of the image signified himself that he set up the image to show off his glory and power.

As grounds for this conjecture, we can cite the fact that a name was not given to the image. If it had been an idol to represent Merodach, it would have been named after Merodach. So I think it was just the nameless golden image Nebuchadnezzar had seen in his dream.

Nebuchadnezzar summoned all the leaders of the empire to the image's dedication. Through that ceremony he intended to show off his glory and consolidate the political unity of his empire.

> *Then the herald loudly proclaimed: "To you the command is given, O peoples, nations and men of every language, that at the moment you hear the sound of the horn, flute, lyre, trigon, psaltery, bagpipe, and all kinds of music, you are to fall down and worship the golden image that Nebuchadnezzar the king has set up. But whoever does not fall down and worship shall immediately be cast into the midst of a furnace of blazing fire." Therefore at that time, when all the peoples heard the sound of the horn, flute, lyre, trigon, psaltery, bagpipe, and all kinds of music, all the peoples, nations and men of every language fell down and worshiped the golden image that Nebuchadnezzar the king had set up (vv. 4-7).*

Today we might think it absurd that the king would command his people to worship an image. But Nebuchadnezzar was the sovereign ruler of the Babylonian empire and held absolute power. Who dared to disobey his command? Neither the king nor his subjects thought that anyone would dare refuse, considering that the punishment for disobedience was to be thrown into a blazing furnace. No wonder all the officials lined up to worship!

And yet not everyone bowed before the image.

Daniel's Friends Refuse to Worship the Idol (3:8-12)

For this reason at that time certain Chaldeans came forward and brought charges against the Jews. They responded and said to Nebuchadnezzar the king: "O king, live forever! You yourself, O king, have made a decree that every man who hears the sound of the horn, flute, lyre, trigon, psaltery, and bagpipe, and all kinds of music, is to fall down and worship the golden image. But whoever does not fall down and worship shall be cast into the midst of a furnace of blazing fire. There are certain Jews whom you have appointed over the administration of the province of Babylon, namely Shadrach, Meshach and Abed-nego. These men, O king, have disregarded you; they do not serve your gods or worship the golden image which you have set up."

Three people in the multitude that day stood upright while everyone else was prostrate. They were Daniel's three friends: Shadrach, Meshach and Abednego. Daniel was saved from the disaster, for he happened to be absent. But his friends could not break God's commandments: "You shall have no other gods before me. You shall not bow down to an idol" (see Ex. 20:3,4). They could keep all the other commands of the king of Babylon, but they could by no means keep any command which was against the laws of God. This was their faith.

Their faith also becomes a great model for Christians today. When the government issues a command, we must obey that command as long as it is not against the commandments of God. There is no authority except that which God has established. It belongs to God to set up a nation and to appoint the one who rules the nation. Therefore, we must submit ourselves to all the governing authorities (see Rom. 13:1).

Nevertheless, when the governing authority forces us to disobey God and compels us to worship an idol, putting other gods in God's place, we must obey God rather than submit ourselves to the worldly power. We must even risk our lives to keep the integrity of our faith.

When Shadrach, Meshach and Abednego obeyed God rather than Nebuchadnezzar, trouble soon came. These Jewish men had been a thorn in the side of the Babylonian nobles because they were foreign exiles who were highly favored by the king. Consequently, the Babylonians had been watching for every opportunity to find fault with them.

Immediately they brought their accusation to the king. And the accusation was not a simple one. They brought three charges against Daniel's friends.

The first accusation was that they did not pay homage to the king. The second accusation was that they did not serve the god of the king. The third accusation was that they did not worship the image the king had set up.

In other words, their accusation was that the Jewish men had no respect for the king, did not serve him and publicly opposed him. Thus their behavior was an infringement upon the sovereignty and authority of the king; in short, it was treason. So for the sake of his dignity and honor, Nebuchadnezzar had to punish the three men.

The Confession of Faith of Daniel's Friends (3:13-18)

Then Nebuchadnezzar in rage and anger gave orders to bring Shadrach, Meshach and Abed-nego; then these men were brought before the king. Nebuchadnezzar responded and said to them, "Is it true, Shadrach, Meshach and Abed-nego, that you do not serve my gods or worship the golden image that I have set up? Now if you are ready, at the moment you hear the sound of the horn, flute, lyre, trigon, psaltery, and bagpipe, and all kinds of music, to fall down and worship the image that I have made, very well. But if you will not worship, you will immediately be cast into the midst of a furnace of blazing fire; and what god is there who can deliver you out of my hands?" (vv. 13-15).

When Nebuchadnezzar thought that his sovereignty was being challenged before his own subjects and the diplomats from foreign kingdoms, his rage knew no bounds. Yet Shadrach, Meshach and Abednego had served as governors of the province for more than fifteen years. During that period they had obtained a good reputation for administration based on wisdom and mercy. If they had been low-level officials, Nebuchadnezzar might have shouted that they should at once be thrown into the furnace. But because they were high-ranking officials who commanded respect both inside and outside his kingdom, Nebuchadnezzar suppressed the surging rage and gave them a second chance.

The king's words to them meant basically this: "In the past the God of the Jewish people revealed to me the interpretation of my dream through Daniel. Yet can he deliver you from the burning furnace?" This was the last chance he could give them and still save face.

The officials and foreign guests in his court were all holding their breath, watching the development of the incident with keen interest. I can imagine that the king's face grew red with anger. Meanwhile, the Babylonians who had accused the three Jews were singing a triumphal song in their hearts.

Shadrach, Meshach and Abed-nego answered and said to the king, "O Nebuchadnezzar, we do not need to give you an answer concerning this matter. If it be so, our God whom we serve is able to deliver us from the furnace of blazing fire; and He will deliver us out of your hand, O king. But even if He does not, let it be known to you, O king, that we are not going to serve your gods or worship the golden image that you have set up" (vv. 16-18).

What a solemn and bold confession of faith this is! Numerous martyrs and saints who suffered persecution in the history of Christianity received great courage from the integrity of faith and bold confession of these three. Their example of faith should inspire and encourage us as well.

The King Becomes Furious (3:19-23)

Then Nebuchadnezzar was filled with wrath, and his facial expression was altered toward Shadrach, Meshach and Abed-nego. He answered by giving orders to heat the furnace seven times more than it was usually heated. And he commanded certain valiant warriors who were in his army to tie up Shadrach, Meshach and Abed-nego, in order to cast them into the furnace of blazing fire. Then these men were tied up in their trousers, their coats, their caps and their other clothes, and were cast into the midst of the furnace of blazing fire. For this reason, because the king's command was urgent and the furnace had been made extremely hot, the flame of the fire slew those men who carried up Shadrach, Meshach and Abed-nego. But these three men, Shadrach, Meshach and Abed-nego, fell into the midst of the furnace of blazing fire still tied up.

When Nebuchadnezzar heard the three Israelites confess their faith, he became so furious that his complexion even changed. Those who stood in the presence of the king all trembled because they knew harm might come to them as well.

Nevertheless, I believe that Shadrach, Meshach and Abed-nego, whose fate hung by a thread, were calm and full of smiles. They were firm in their faith that God could easily deliver them from the burning furnace. Their solemn attitude showed that, even if it were not God's will to deliver them, they could never be brought to worship the image.

These three men truly loved God. Their great love of God made them ready to die for God rather than lose the integrity of their faith. What we should learn from them is this: Even if the same crisis should come to us, forcing us to acknowledge Jesus at the cost of our lives, we should never waiver in the confession of our faith.

In the journey of life we sometimes fall into sin because of our weakness. But if we come back to God and repent of our sins, He forgives us. When we compromise in this area, breaking the commandment "You shall have no other gods before me," God is grieved and angry, because this is a matter which concerns His majesty.

For that reason, when we are put to the test by those who would demand that we worship another god, we must never compromise. Rather we must resist even at the risk of our own lives. This is the fundamental reason Christians have never been able to embrace that now-faltering ideology called communism. Communists deny the existence of God and worship their ideology as god. So we cannot make any concessions to communism, but instead must continue to fight against it, no matter what the cost.

Anger Leads to Foolishness

In his rage Nebuchadnezzar shouted at his subjects, "Heat up the furnace seven times hotter than usual!" Anger is always accompanied by such foolishness. In calmness of heart we can say wise words, while in anger we utter foolish ones.

Here Nebuchadnezzar's rage made him a fool because his command was counterproductive. If he had wanted to maximize the pain of the three men, he should have lowered the heat of the furnace so that it would not kill them instantly. But he did the opposite.

Full of anger, Nebuchadnezzar continued to speak foolish words and do foolish things. Notice that the king commanded the three men to be thrown into the *midst* of the blazing furnace. If the three men had been thrown into the *mouth* of the furnace, that would have served the purpose just as well. It was just a decision made in anger.

In order to carry out this command of the king, several soldiers had to raise the three men one by one and throw them. The result was the unfair death of several soldiers who were consumed by the fire while trying to carry out the command. Thus the king's anger led not only to foolishness but finally to tragedy.

Though this is but a small example, here is an important lesson we must realize: We must not under any circumstances make decisions in anger. A decision made in anger leads to failure.

The Fourth Man (3:24-27)

Then Nebuchadnezzar the king was astounded and stood up in haste; he responded and said to his high officials, "Was it not three men we cast bound into the midst of the fire?" They answered and said to the king, "Certainly, O king." He answered and said, "Look! I see four men loosed and walking about in the midst of the fire without harm, and the appearance of the fourth is like a son of the gods!" Then Nebuchadnezzar came near to the door of the furnace of blazing fire; he responded and said, "Shadrach, Meshach and Abed-nego, come out, you servants of the Most High God, and come here!" Then Shadrach, Meshach and Abed-nego came out of the midst of the fire. And the satraps, the prefects, the governors and the king's high officials gathered around and saw in regard to these men that the fire had no effect on the bodies of these men nor was the hair of their head singed, nor were their trousers damaged, nor had the smell of fire even come upon them.

Once the three men were thrown into the furnace by the command of Nebuchadnezzar—the king of Babylon, who held such power that he dictated to the world—everyone including the king himself assumed that the three men died. But the man who is with God does not die. Only the ropes binding the three men were burned up by the fire.

The rope is a symbol of royal power dominating the whole world. Only that symbol of power was burned up like bits of straw, while Shadrach, Meshach and Abednego danced in the midst of the fire. Then Nebuchadnezzar saw a fourth man like "a son of the gods" dancing with them in the fire and was astonished (v. 25).

Human beings cannot obstruct what God does. God was watching this scene in heaven, and He also heard the unyielding confession of faith spoken by Shadrach, Meshach and Abednego.

You see, Nebuchadnezzar used the expression ''a son of the gods'' not knowing who the man was. But the fourth man in the fire was Jesus Christ. As the men had been dragged to the furnace, the Son must have said to the Father, ''Father, I will go down to the earth. We cannot let these who have such uncompromising faith die. We must show them that the God of the universe lives.'' Then, when Shadrach, Meshach and Abednego fell into the fire at the command of the furious Nebuchadnezzar, the Son of God had also jumped into the fire.

What is impossible to the God who made heaven and earth? Just as He would later command the physical elements and cause the furious storm to become calm, He took charge of the fire and commanded it to do no harm to God's children, however hotly it burned.

This story should remind us that when we suffer persecution we meet Jesus. If we stand before the Lord with uncompromising faith, this fourth man, Jesus Christ, will always be with us: ''Lo, I am with you always, even to the end of the age'' (Matt. 28:20). Even today God wants to deliver us miraculously out of the fire.

A Royal Summons

Nebuchadnezzar was struck dumb with amazement to see that the rope, which was a symbol of his power, honor and dignity, had been burned up, while the three men he had ordered executed were running around free. He discovered that his power and authority did not originate with himself, but with God.

Not one sparrow will fall to the ground apart from the will

of God. When Pilate asked Jesus, "Don't you realize I have power either to free you or to crucify you?" Jesus answered, "You would have no power over me except what is given to you from above" (see John 19:10,11). Neither Pilate nor Nebuchadnezzar nor any other ruler has any power over God's people except what God has allowed them to have.

When the king and his officials realized what had happened, the king's rage turned to fear. With a trembling voice he summoned them to come out, calling them "servants of the most high God" (v. 26).

When the three men heard this, they came out immediately, and the fourth man disappeared. They obeyed this command to come out even though the king had had them thrown into the furnace, because the power to rule the kingdom of Babylon was nevertheless given by God. Although they could by no means obey the royal command to worship an idol in opposition to God's commandment, they still obeyed the other commands given by the king because it was their duty as the king's subjects according to the will of God.

We also should follow the example of their attitude. While we live in this world, we preach the gospel with all our might and try to change our environment according to our vision of success. But we also have a duty to submit ourselves to the government we have elected.

Of course, if an official commands us to betray God, we must resist unto death. Yet otherwise we must submit to and pray for the political leaders of our country. They are human beings just as we are, so we must help them with our prayers that they may receive God's wisdom and understanding to lead the nation.

When Shadrach, Meshach and Abednego came out of the furnace, the king and his officials crowded around them to touch their clothes and their bodies. Seeing that the fire had not harmed them, they were further amazed to discover that even the smell of fire was not on them. The king wondered, "How on earth could such a thing be possible?"

Nebuchadnezzar Praises God (3:28-30)

Nebuchadnezzar responded and said, "Blessed be the God of Shadrach, Meshach and Abed-nego, who has sent His angel and delivered His servants who put their trust in Him, violating the king's command, and yielded up their bodies so as not to serve or worship any god except their own God. Therefore, I make a decree that any people, nation or tongue that speaks anything offensive against the God of Shadrach, Meshach and Abed-nego shall be torn limb from limb and their houses reduced to a rubbish heap, inasmuch as there is no other god who is able to deliver in this way." Then the king caused Shadrach, Meshach and Abed-nego to prosper in the province of Babylon.

Nebuchadnezzar at last praised the one true God. He even went so far as to threaten anyone who spoke against God in his kingdom.

Notice here that in the king's thinking God had become the God of Shadrach, Meshach and Abednego—the personal God of these men. In a similar way the Bible says that God was the God of Abraham, Isaac and Jacob, for He was the God experienced personally by each of these patriarchs throughout their lives.

God wants to become your personal God as well. You should live your life in such a way that other people will speak of God as *your* God. Let them put your own name behind His. When the living God comes into your own life to work so that you experience Him personally, signs and wonders will appear.

Notice as well that even though Nebuchadnezzar decreed that no one should speak anything against God, he still did not say that everyone should believe in God. This is an indication that he still had pride in his heart. Later, however, we will see him completely yielding to God and confessing that everyone should believe in Him.

What was the result of this episode with the furnace? The king promoted Shadrach, Meshach and Abednego. Consequently, the whole kingdom of Babylon came to serve a handful of Jewish exiles as their masters. Daniel and his three friends took all the key posts of the court.

This story illustrates vividly that when God is with us we become the head, wherever we may be. So we don't need to worry, because in all things God works for the good of those who love Him (see Rom. 8:28).

4

Nebuchadnezzar's Insanity and Recovery

Nebuchadnezzar's Second Dream (4:1-3)

Nebuchadnezzar the king to all the peoples, nations, and men of every language that live in all the earth: "May your peace abound! It has seemed good to me to declare the signs and wonders which the Most High God has done for me.
How great are His signs,
And how mighty are His wonders!
His kingdom is an everlasting kingdom,
And His dominion is from generation to generation."

Time and again God gave His revelation to King Nebuchadnezzar through dreams. In Daniel chapter 2, through the dream of the golden image, God showed him what would happen in the future of the world, and Daniel interpreted the dream for him clearly.

Chapter 4 is set in the context of Nebuchadnezzar's decree telling about a judgment by God that resulted in the king's becoming insane for seven years. When Nebuchadnezzar had finally recovered, he was so overwhelmed with gratitude that he issued the decree giving praise to God.

The King Relies on Daniel for the Interpretation (4:4-9)

"I, Nebuchadnezzar, was at ease in my house and flourishing in my palace. I saw a dream and it made me fearful; and these fantasies as I lay on my bed and the visions in my mind kept alarming me. So I gave orders to bring into my presence all the wise men of Babylon, that they might make known to me the interpretation of the dream. Then the magicians, the conjurers, the Chaldeans, and the diviners came in, and I related the dream to them; but they could not make its interpretation known to me. But finally Daniel came in before me, whose name is Belteshazzar according to the name of my god, and in whom is a spirit of the holy gods; and I related the dream to him, saying, 'O Belteshazzar, chief of the magicians, since I know that a spirit of the holy gods is in you and no mystery baffles you, tell me the visions of my dream which I have seen, along with its interpretation.' "

We can conclude that even a wicked man like Nebuchadnezzar was broken enough in heart to believe in God, considering that he appointed a man like Daniel as chief of governors—a man with a pure faith of integrity who met with God every morning and evening. Our influence as believers is greater than we realize. This is why Paul says, "For the unbelieving husband is sanctified through his wife, and the unbelieving wife is sanctified through her believing husband" (1 Cor. 7:14). The marriage relationship represents the greatest influence of this kind. Accordingly, when one spouse has faith, the other is necessarily affected.

The influence of a Christian is like the mustard seed. It looks small, but when the seed is sown it grows to become a big tree. Our influence is also like yeast. Only a little bit of yeast in a large wooden kneading bowl is enough to leaven the whole dough.

Under the influence of Daniel's faith, the stubborn and wicked man Nebuchadnezzar became a new man after he had recovered from his insanity. His unbelief was completely broken, and he became a worshipper of God. The greeting at the beginning of his decree and the peals of praise to God that follow even resemble those in the New Testament epistles of that great man of faith, the apostle Paul: "May your peace abound!...How great are His signs and how mighty are His wonders!" (v. 1,3).

One primary concern of a heathen ruler was to establish his kingdom and to preserve the throne for his posterity from generation to generation. But instead Nebuchadnezzar confessed that *God's* kingdom "is an everlasting kingdom, and His dominion is from generation to generation" (v. 3).

This is an extraordinary transformation. Nebuchadnezzar had been responsible for the fall of Israel. He had sent an army to overthrow the nation and to destroy the temple of God. Yet through Daniel, an exile whom he had brought to his court, he came to believe in God and to praise Him.

This is the power of faith. When Jesus heard Peter confess faith in Him, He said, "Upon this rock I will build My church; and the gates of Hades shall not overpower it" (Matt. 16:18). Who is this rock? He is the person who confesses as Peter did, "Thou art the Christ, the Son of the living God" (Matt. 16:16). Anyone who believes and confesses today "Thou art the Christ, the Son of the living God" is the same kind of rock, and upon this rock Jesus builds His church.

Furthermore, Jesus referred to Himself as the stone and said, "He who falls on this stone will be broken to pieces; but on whomever it falls, it will scatter him like dust" (Matt 21:44). Jesus dwells in you and me. So when unbelievers "bump" against believers, they are spiritually broken to pieces and are brought to repentance.

Of course, we are speaking here of the kind of Christian who lives faithfully, having Jesus at the center of his or her life. Sadly enough, there is another kind of Christian who leads a worse life than a non-Christian, though he or she may profess faith in Jesus Christ. Such a person is a shame to Him.

The Bible says, "Faith, if it has no works, is dead, being by itself" (James 2:17) and "You shall love your neighbor as yourself" (Matt. 22:39). To love God and your neighbor are the basic principles of Christianity.

Why does the Bible emphasize faith with works? Through faith at work, we can let our neighbors see God. King Nebuchadnezzar of heathen Babylon saw the God of Shadrach, Meshach, Abednego and Daniel. Because of their faith at work, he could become like these children of God.

The same is true today. People around us are watching us. Whether we are an elder or a senior deaconess or a deacon, whether we are a home cell group leader or a church member without any leadership responsibilities, they are observing our behavior. They want to see God in us.

In the midst of this world with all its problems there is no one to turn to, so they want to believe in our God. Show them God, as Daniel and his friends did. Through faith and behavior worthy of the name of God's children, show them God their creator. "Let your light shine before men in such a way that they may see your good works, and glorify your Father who is in heaven'' (Matt. 5:16).

For the glory of Christ, this should be the attitude of a Christian: If someone forces us to go one mile, we should go two; if someone wants to take our tunic, we should let him have our cloak as well; if someone strikes us on the right cheek, we should turn to him the other also (see Matt. 5:39-41). In the eyes of the people in the world, these behaviors may seem to make us losers. But since God is for us, who can be against us (see Rom. 8:31)? We will have God as our strength, and He will bless us.

Therefore, we must diligently learn the pattern Daniel set forth. His faith had such integrity that it even impressed the pagan King Nebuchadnezzar and showed him God. In this way, through the quality of his life Daniel was an excellent preacher of God. I pray in the name of Jesus that you too may become a precious saint like Daniel who reflects God in your daily life.

The Contents of the Dream (4:10-18)

" 'Now these were the visions in my mind as I lay on
my bed: I was looking, and behold, there was a tree
in the midst of the earth, and its height was great.
   The tree grew large and became strong,
   And its height reached to the sky,
   And it was visible to the end of the whole earth.
   Its foliage was beautiful and its fruit abundant,
   And in it was food for all.
   The beasts of the field found shade under it,
   And the birds of the sky dwelt in its branches,
   And all living creatures fed themselves from it' "
(vv. 10-12).

Up to this point the king's dream must have been pleasant

and hardly worth his calling in the interpreters to examine. But suddenly the dream became a nightmare.

" 'I was looking in the visions in my mind as I lay on my bed, and behold, an angelic watcher, a holy one, descended from heaven. He shouted out and spoke as follows:

"Chop down the tree and cut off its branches,
Strip off its foliage and scatter its fruit;
Let the beasts flee from under it,
And the birds from its branches.
Yet leave the stump with its roots in the ground,
But with a band of iron and bronze around it
In the new grass of the field;
And let him be drenched with the dew of heaven,
And let him share with the beasts in the grass of the earth.
Let his mind be changed from that of a man,
And let a beast's mind be given to him,
And let seven periods of time pass over him.
This sentence is by the decree of the angelic watchers,
And the decision is a command of the holy ones,
In order that the living may know
That the Most High is ruler over the realm of mankind,
And bestows it on whom He wishes,
And sets over it the lowliest of men."
'This is the dream which I, King Nebuchadnezzar, have seen. Now you, Belteshazzar, tell me its interpretation, inasmuch as none of the wise men of my kingdom is able to make known to me the interpretation; but you are able, for a spirit of the holy gods is in you' " (vv. 13-18).

The voice from heaven, like thunder, disturbed the peaceful-ness of the dream, and Nebuchadnezzar was terrified. When he awoke he knew it was a divine revelation. So he called for all the magicians, enchanters and astrologers of Babylon for an interpretation. But none of them could do it, because demons cannot interpret a divine revelation.

We should keep this in mind as we pray. When we pray in our common language, our prayer is understood by both God and the devil. But when we pray in tongues, our prayer is understood by no one but God unless God gives an interpreta-tion: "For one who speaks in tongues does not speak to men, but to God; for no one understands, but in his spirit he speaks mysteries" (1 Cor. 14:2).

For that reason, if we are filled with the Holy Spirit and can pray in tongues, we should endeavor to pray that way often. It is the prayer our spirits offer directly to God, and it brings us great benefit.

Daniel's Interpretation (4:19-27)

"Then Daniel, whose name is Belteshazzar, was ap-palled for a while as his thoughts alarmed him. The king responded and said, 'Belteshazzar, do not let the dream or its interpretation alarm you.' Belteshazzar answered and said, 'My lord, if only the dream applied to those who hate you, and its interpretation to your adver-saries!' " (v. 19).

When none of the magicians and the enchanters was able to interpret the dream for him, Nebuchadnezzar called for Daniel. But when Daniel learned the meaning of the dream, he was so terrified that he was mute for a time. The king had to en-courage Daniel not to worry but to tell the interpretation of the dream. Comforted by this, Daniel began to interpret the dream, wishing that the thing would not happen to the king.

" 'The tree that you saw, which became large and grew strong, whose height reached to the sky and was visible to all the earth, and whose foliage was beautiful and its fruit abundant, and in which was food for all, under which the beasts of the field dwelt and in whose branches the birds of the sky lodged—it is you, O king; for you have become great and grown strong, and your majesty has become great and reached to the sky and your dominion to the end of the earth' " (vv. 20-22).

So far the interpretation was complimentary rather than troubling. But then Daniel went on.

" 'And in that the king saw an angelic watcher, a holy one, descending from heaven and saying, "Chop down the tree and destroy it; yet leave the stump with its roots in the ground, but with a band of iron and bronze around it in the new grass of the field, and let him be drenched with the dew of heaven, and let him share with the beasts of the field until seven periods of time pass over him"; this is the interpretation, O king, and this is the decree of the Most High, which has come upon my lord the king: that you be driven away from mankind, and your dwelling place be with the beasts of the field, and you be given grass to eat like cattle and be drenched with the dew of heaven; and seven periods of time will pass over you, until you recognize that the Most High is ruler over the realm of mankind, and bestows it on whomever He wishes. And in that it was commanded to leave the stump with the roots of the tree, your kingdom will be assured to you after you recognize that it is Heaven that rules' "

(vv. 23-26).

To summarize: Daniel first revealed that the tree represented Nebuchadnezzar. Next he said that the one who came down from heaven was a divine messenger and his words told what would happen to the king; namely, that the king would be insane for seven years and would live in the field eating grass like cattle, having been driven from the royal palace. Then, said Daniel, the king's pride would be broken, and he would acknowledge the sovereignty of God. Afterward, the king would be brought back to his throne.

> " 'Therefore, O king, may my advice be pleasing to you:
> break away now from your sins by doing righteousness,
> and from your iniquities by showing mercy to the poor,
> in case there may be a prolonging of your prosperity' "
> *(v. 27).*

Next Daniel gave advice to the king. He said that Nebuchadnezzar should change his ways and act righteously.

We should keep in mind that it was hard to find righteousness in the kings of that day. They had such absolute power that they could seize the possessions of their subjects on a whim, and they even held the power of life and death over them. Their tyranny knew no limits.

Nebuchadnezzar had used his power to mobilize a large number of poor people in forced labor to build the city of Babylon. They had been terribly mistreated. Under such circumstances, Daniel advised the king to cease from oppressing these poor people.

Nebuchadnezzar's Pride (4:28-30)

"All this happened to Nebuchadnezzar the king. Twelve months later he was walking on the roof of the royal

59

palace of Babylon. The king reflected and said, 'Is this not Babylon the great, which I myself have built as a royal residence by the might of my power and for the glory of my majesty?' "

Next Nebuchadnezzar described what actually happened to him. Twelve months after he had dreamed the dream, the king went out on the flat, spacious roof of the palace and looked down upon the city of Babylon.

The sight of the city which spread before him near and far must have been impressive and beautiful. Modern archeologists who excavated the site of Babylon say that it was one of the architectural wonders of the world's ancient civilizations, a magnificent city built by the hard labor of people enslaved from the countries Babylon conquered.

Looking out over such a sight, the king proudly threw back his shoulders and boasted about it. What he said was similar to Satan's proud words when he rebelled against God. Being puffed up, the devil claimed:

"I will ascend to heaven;
I will raise my throne above the stars of God,
And I will sit on the mount of assembly
In the recesses of the north.
I will ascend above the heights of the clouds;
I will make myself like the Most High" (Is. 14:13,14).

Because of his proud rebellion Satan fell from heaven and into hell. The Bible says, "Pride goes before destruction, and a haughty spirit before stumbling" (Prov. 16:18). God brings the arrogant low and exalts the humble-hearted—not only among His chosen people, but among the heathen as well. So we should not be surprised that God humbled this man and that the king's pride led to his downfall.

The King's Heart Is Changed (4:31-33)

As soon as Nebuchadnezzar uttered those arrogant words on the roof of the palace, he heard a voice from heaven:

> *"While the word was in the king's mouth, a voice came from heaven, saying, 'King Nebuchadnezzar, to you it is declared: sovereignty has been removed from you, and you will be driven away from mankind, and your dwelling place will be with the beasts of the field. You will be given grass to eat like cattle, and seven periods of time will pass over you, until you recognize that the Most High is ruler over the realm of mankind, and bestows it on whomever He wishes.' "* (vv. 31,32).

No sooner had these words been spoken than the human heart departed from Nebuchadnezzar, and the heart of a beast was given to him instead.

> *"Immediately the word concerning Nebuchadnezzar was fulfilled; and he was driven away from mankind and began eating grass like cattle, and his body was drenched with the dew of heaven, until his hair had grown like eagles' feathers and his nails like birds' claws"* (v. 33).

The total transformation of a human heart can be tragic, as in the case of this king. Yet the change can take another direction as well, bringing great benefit. For example, when John the Baptist preached, he said, "Repent, for the kingdom of heaven is at hand" (Matt. 3:2). Here the biblical Greek word for "repent" means "to change the thoughts of one's heart"—a change that leads to salvation.

The condition of our hearts is important because our hearts determine our behavior. If people dwell on murder in their hearts, they will eventually commit murder. If lewd thinking creeps into their hearts, they will sooner or later translate it into sexually immoral action.

On the other hand, if their hearts are sanctified, their behavior will be sanctified, too. If they have faith in their hearts, they will behave accordingly. If their hearts become positive and prosperous, actions that bring them success and victory will necessarily follow.

The heart must be changed before the life can be changed. And a change of environment does not necessarily bring a change of heart. Instead, a change of heart will bring a change of environment.

The Bible says, "Watch over your heart with all diligence, for from it flow the springs of life" (Prov. 4:23). The heart must be kept in such a way that pride cannot possess it. And a bad heart must be renewed by the blood of Jesus Christ to become a good one.

When we repent and change our hearts in Jesus Christ through hearing the Word of God, our lives become totally different. That is why the apostle Paul said, "Therefore if any man is in Christ, he is a new creature; the old things passed away; behold, new things have come" (2 Cor. 5:17). If we are born again to become positive, active and creative people, and if we fill our hearts with things which are rich and victorious according to the Word of God, our lives and even our environment will bear the same fruit.

For that reason, keep the Holy Spirit always in your heart and let Him be the master of it. Fill your heart with the Word of God so that your faith may grow. Your environment will also be changed beautifully in proportion to the growth of your faith.

Nebuchadnezzar Recognizes God's Sovereignty (4:34-37)

"But at the end of that period I, Nebuchadnezzar, raised my eyes toward heaven, and my reason returned to me, and I blessed the Most High and praised and honored Him who lives forever;

For His dominion is an everlasting dominion,
And His kingdom endures from generation to generation.
And all the inhabitants of the earth are accounted as nothing,
But He does according to His will in the host of heaven
And among the inhabitants of earth;
And no one can ward off His hand
Or say to Him, 'What hast Thou done?'

"At that time my reason returned to me. And my majesty and splendor were restored to me for the glory of my kingdom, and my counselors and my nobles began seeking me out; so I was reestablished in my sovereignty, and surpassing greatness was added to me" (vv. 34-36).

When we read that Nebuchadnezzar raised his eyes toward heaven, we can understand this to mean that he surrendered himself to God and came to admit the sovereignty of God. He fully realized now that God could exalt him or bring him low; that God was able to spare his life or destroy it.

Then the heart of the beast left him, and his sanity was restored. He bowed down to God and prayed, giving thanks and praise. And he committed his life to the sovereign God.

When he had recovered, a group of his subjects headed by Daniel brought him back to the throne and once more served him as the king. In fact, Daniel was responsible for ensuring that Nebuchadnezzar was able to return to his throne after an absence of seven years.

Daniel's prophecy had been heard by all the people in the court. They knew from his words that the king's insanity was temporary, that he would return to rule and that the whole episode happened by divine providence. If Daniel had not prophesied this, King Nebuchadnezzar would have died. His enemies would have followed the insane man to the field and killed him to usurp the throne. But because Daniel prophesied what God would do, no one dared to attempt an assassination. They were afraid of Daniel's prophecy and of the God whom he worshipped.

> *"Now I Nebuchadnezzar praise, exalt, and honor the King of heaven, for all His works are true and His ways just, and He is able to humble those who walk in pride"* (v. 37).

Here at last Nebuchadnezzar has repented of his arrogance. Acknowledging God's sovereignty, he has become a man who trusts in God.

Notice here an important point: Even such a wicked and ruthless man as King Nebuchadnezzar fell by Daniel's prayer and became one of God's people. From a merely human perspective, the prayers offered by Daniel may have seemed as futile an effort as trying to sweep the sea with a broom. Nevertheless, this terrible king of a heathen kingdom who had previously worshipped Merodach, believing that he was above all gods, surrendered himself at last to the true God. This transformation speaks for the patience of Daniel's prayers.

We should remember Daniel's example. Even though we sometimes seem to receive no immediate answer to our prayers, we shouldn't lose heart. Daniel did not receive the answer to his prayers even within a year or two. He had to pray constantly for King Nebuchadnezzar for twenty years.

Our prayers are bound to be answered. So pray in bold faith. As the Scripture says, "Believe in the Lord Jesus, and you shall be saved, you and your household" (Acts 16:31). Do not cease praying for the redemption of the members of your family. Even that ruthless heathen Nebuchadnezzar surrendered. How much more will your relatives? I pray in Jesus' name that you may pray for them in faith and finally receive the answer you desire.

5

Belshazzar's Banquet

The Desecration of the Temple Vessels (5:1-4)

Belshazzar the king held a great feast for a thousand of his nobles, and he was drinking wine in the presence of the thousand. When Belshazzar tasted the wine, he gave orders to bring the gold and silver vessels which Nebuchadnezzar his father had taken out of the temple which was in Jerusalem, in order that the king and his nobles, his wives, and his concubines might drink from them. Then they brought the gold vessels that had been taken out of the temple, the house of God which was in Jerusalem; and the king and his nobles, his wives, and his concubines drank from them. They drank the wine and praised the gods of gold and silver, of bronze, iron, wood, and stone.

In this text Nebuchadnezzar is called Belshazzar's father, but actually he was Belshazzar's grandfather. In the Aramaic language the word we translate "father" frequently meant "ancestor," and "son" often meant "descendant."

King Belshazzar was a viceroy of his father, Nabonidas, who was at the oasis city of Tema, recuperating from mental illness.

At that time Darius, the king of Media, came with a Medo-Persian army of irresistible force to besiege Babylon. But Babylon was an adamant city, enormous and strongly built. Since the city also had provisions for several years in preparation for such a siege, it refused to yield. Furthermore, because the Euphrates River ran beneath the city, Babylon seemed invincible.

Even so, King Belshazzar was restless. He feared that the soldiers and even the generals of his army might be demoralized while the city was under siege for such a long time. The king racked his brain to solve this problem and finally decided to give a banquet for his subjects to pacify them. So he prepared a great feast for one thousand of his nobles.

When he had gotten drunk, a foolish idea came into his mind. He commanded his servants to bring forth the vessels of gold and silver which had formerly been used in the sacrifices to God at the temple in Jerusalem—vessels which his ancestor King Nebuchadnezzar had taken as spoils. Then Belshazzar and the others present drank wine from them in the name of their pagan gods.

This was a blasphemous desecration. Nebuchadnezzar himself had not even dared to touch them, much less do such a thing. But Belshazzar was so drunk that he became foolish and forgot the fear of God. How then could God ignore what they had done?

In the Bible we see that when people violated any of the last six of the Ten Commandments—those regulating human relationships—God forgave them and gave them opportunity for repentance. But when people violated any of the first four commandments, which dealt with their relationship to God, God's judgment often came more quickly. No wonder then that the judgment of Belshazzar and his guests was swift.

Japan's defeat in World War II is a good example of this truth. During the war, the emperor of Japan proclaimed that World War II was the war between the Japanese god of Amateras and the God of the Christians. Because Japan had thus profaned the holiness of God, God made that nation the victim of a horrible atomic bombing, and it finally had to surrender.

Likewise, the Nazi leader Adolf Hitler proudly claimed that later history would record him as a god, if there was any such being like a god. And God struck him down.

For decades now the communists have been arrogant. They have blasphemed God and denied His existence. They have devastated the churches, prohibited education about God and forbidden the worship of God. So we are not surprised to be seeing now in our generation the downfall of communism and its disappearance from this stage in history—for they have attacked the very nature of God.

God still forgives all the faults Christians commit against their brothers and sisters. But if they pull down the church, which is the body of Christ, God swiftly judges them. When Ananias and Sapphira, for example, tried to deceive God and the church by keeping some money to themselves, God struck them dead on the spot (Acts 5:1-11). For this reason, we should always examine our relationship with God to find anything amiss before Him.

Of course, as for the fourth commandment that regards the Sabbath day, Jesus said, "The Son of Man is Lord of the Sabbath" (Matt. 12:8). So to us who believe in our Lord Jesus Christ, every day is the Sabbath day. And the day when Jesus Christ was resurrected is the Lord's day, so we must keep it holy. Consequently, the Bible says that we should not let anyone judge us with regard to the Sabbath day (Col. 2:16).

If, however, we violate any of the other three commandments dealing with our relationship to God—"You shall have no other gods before Me," "You shall not make for yourself an idol," "You shall not take the name of your God in vain"—immediate judgment will come upon us. Not only Christians but also non-Christians will be judged if they violate any of those commandments. So even though you may fall and make mistakes in other aspects of your faith life, never violate any of those first three commandments.

The Divine Judgment (5:5-12)

Suddenly the fingers of a man's hand emerged and began writing opposite the lampstand on the plaster of the wall of the king's palace, and the king saw the back of the hand that did the writing. Then the king's face grew pale, and his thoughts alarmed him; and his hip joints went slack, and his knees began knocking together. The king called aloud to bring in the conjurers, the Chaldeans and the diviners. The king spoke and said to the wise men of Babylon, "Any man who can read this inscription and explain its interpretation to me will be clothed with purple, and have a necklace of gold around his neck, and have authority as third ruler in the kingdom." Then all the king's wise men came in, but they could not read the inscription or make known its interpretation to the king. Then King Belshazzar was greatly alarmed, his face grew even paler, and his nobles were perplexed (vv. 5-9).

As soon as King Belshazzar profaned the vessels of the

temple, the divine judgment was given. In the middle of the merrymaking, suddenly there was heard a sharp shriek: "Look at that wall!"

Belshazzar evidently sensed that the handwriting he saw there was an ill omen and may even have guessed that it had to do with his act of desecration. Since he was a viceroy to his father, his offer to make the interpreter of the message the third highest ruler in the kingdom meant he was offering the position of chief administrator, immediately below himself—so concerned was he to understand what was written.

His fear understandably increased all the more when none of his wise men could interpret the writing. As we said before, they were unable to help him because demons cannot interpret a revelation from God.

> *The queen entered the banquet hall because of the words of the king and his nobles; the queen spoke and said, "O king, live forever! Do not let your thoughts alarm you or your face be pale. There is a man in your kingdom in whom is a spirit of the holy gods; and in the days of your father, illumination, insight, and wisdom like the wisdom of the gods were found in him. And King Nebuchadnezzar, your father, your father the king, appointed him chief of the magicians, conjurers, Chaldeans, and diviners. This was because an extraordinary spirit, knowledge and insight, interpretation of dreams, explanation of enigmas, and solving of difficult problems were found in this Daniel, whom the king named Belteshazzar. Let Daniel now be summoned, and he will declare the interpretation" (vv. 10-12).*

Amid the chaos of the banquet, the shouts of the king and the murmuring of the guests, the queen entered and spoke wise advice: Call Daniel. Evidently Daniel was living in retirement at that time, having withdrawn from active politics because of his old age.

Daniel's Interpretation (5:13-31)

Then Daniel was brought in before the king. The king spoke and said to Daniel, "Are you that Daniel who is one of the exiles from Judah, whom my father the king brought from Judah? Now I have heard about you that a spirit of the gods is in you, and that illumination, insight, and extraordinary wisdom have been found in you. Just now the wise men and the conjurers were brought in before me that they might read this inscription and make its interpretation known to me, but they could not declare the interpretation of the message. But I personally have heard about you, that you are able to give interpretations and solve difficult problems. Now if you are able to read the inscription and make its interpretation known to me, you will be clothed with purple and wear a necklace of gold around your neck, and you will have authority as the third ruler in the kingdom." Then Daniel answered and said before the king, "Keep your gifts for yourself, or give your rewards to someone else; however, I will read the inscription to the king and make the interpretation known to him" (vv. 13-17).

Receiving the royal order, Daniel came in hurriedly. Notice that though the king gave to Daniel the same promises of wealth and promotion he had given the others, Daniel turned them down. He already knew from the contents of the writing that such promises were meaningless, because the end of Babylon was imminent.

Instead, Daniel, though only a Jewish exile, gave a bold history lecture to the heathen king of Babylon, the world power of that day. Now that Daniel was quite old, he had no lingering affection for anything but to serve God. Nor was he afraid of death. Therefore he sharply rebuked King Belshazzar. He said:

"O king, the Most High God granted sovereignty, grandeur, glory, and majesty to Nebuchadnezzar your father. And because of the grandeur which He bestowed on him, all the peoples, nations, and men of every language feared and trembled before him; whomever he wished he killed, and whomever he wished he spared alive; and whomever he wished he elevated, and whomever he wished he humbled. But when his heart was lifted up and his spirit became so proud that he behaved arrogantly, he was deposed from his royal throne, and his glory was taken away from him. He was also driven away from mankind, and his heart was made like that of beasts, and his dwelling place was with the wild donkeys. He was given grass to eat like cattle, and his body was drenched with the dew of heaven, until he recognized that the Most High God is ruler over the realm of mankind, and that He sets over it whomever He wishes. Yet you, his son, Belshazzar, have not humbled your heart, even though you knew all this, but you have exalted yourself against the Lord of heaven; and they have brought the vessels of His house before you, and you and your nobles, your wives and your concubines have been drinking wine from them; and you have praised the gods of silver and gold, of bronze, iron, wood and stone, which do not see, hear or understand. But the God in whose hand are your life-breath and your

ways, you have not glorified. Then the hand was sent from Him, and this inscription was written out" (vv. 18-24).

Don't you know, he was saying, what happened to your father—how God humbled him? You are his blood relative and saw it with your own eyes. Haven't you learned your lesson yet? No! Far from learning a lesson, you even blasphemed God by drinking wine from the sacred vessels. Therefore God will judge you. Now there is no time even for repentance. That writing on the wall forebodes an impending judgment!

When Daniel finished lecturing to Belshazzar, Babylon was already doomed and without hope. God had opened the way of forgiveness to King Nebuchadnezzar, but to King Belshazzar he did not give a chance to repent. Though Nebuchadnezzar's pride caused him to undergo divine "training" for seven years during his insanity, he nevertheless did not blaspheme God as Belshazzar did. But because Belshazzar blasphemed God, the Holy Spirit left him and the way of forgiveness for him was closed.

The Bible says that all the sins of people will be forgiven except one: Whoever blasphemes against the Holy Spirit will not be forgiven both in this world and in the world to come (Mark 3:29). The sin of blaspheming against the Holy Spirit is the sin a person commits by calling the work of the Holy Spirit the work of a demon out of envy and jealousy, even though that person knows it is the work of the Spirit. If a person calls the Holy Spirit a demon, the Holy Spirit leaves that person.

I once knew a man who blasphemed against the Holy Spirit and was forsaken by Him. He and I were saved together in the city of Pusan in Korea, and we both preached on the streets. He was such a Spirit-filled man that everybody called him Holy

Ghost Boy. Many people envied him and wished to be filled with the Holy Spirit as he was.

Later I came to Seoul to become a pastor, but he went out into the world. Worse yet, he blasphemed against the Holy Spirit by saying that the things he had experienced up to that time were not the works of the Holy Spirit, but the works of a demon. So the Holy Spirit left him.

When he went into the army, he did all the wicked things of the devil. Later, however, he was tormented with an extreme agony of heart as if he had been in hell. It seemed that he could hardly bear the pain. So he called on me when I was pastoring my church in the city of Seodaemun.

This man opened his heart to me then and said that he had been writhing with agony of heart. I can still remember his words: "Pastor Cho, for God's sake, help me! As an old friend, have pity on me and make me get out of this pain. Though I have tried hard, I can neither repent of my sin nor believe in Jesus again. My heart seems to be burning and my soul seems to be in hell several thousand miles away from me. For God's sake help me!"

So I took hold of him and did everything I could do to help him repent, only to fail. The Spirit had already left him.

"No one can say, 'Jesus is Lord,' except by the Holy Spirit" (1 Cor. 12:3). If we believe in Jesus and confess that Jesus is our Lord while the Holy Spirit dwells in our hearts, we can repent of our sins, and they will be forgiven. When the Spirit leaves us, however, there will be no more chances. Such was the state in which King Belshazzar found himself. The hour of destruction came, but he could not find a way out.

Today all who do not have Jesus will find themselves in the same situation. Now is the age of grace when whoever repents of sin and confesses that Jesus is the Lord will be saved.

"Behold, now is 'the acceptable time,' behold, now is 'the day of salvation' " (2 Cor. 6:2).

But all who reject such an opportunity for salvation will later stand before the judgment seat of Jesus and hear the stern voice of the Lord condemning them. By that time the hand will have already written the judgment on the wall. There will be no hope. Only the eternal pain of hell will be waiting. So I pray in Jesus' name that you will never forsake Jesus once you believe in Him.

After his "history lecture," Daniel read the writing on the wall and interpreted its meaning:

"Now this is the inscription that was written out: 'MENE, MENE, TEKEL, UPHARSIN.' This is the interpretation of the message: 'MENE'—God has numbered your kingdom and put an end to it. 'TEKEL'— you have been weighed on the scales and found deficient. 'PERES'—your kingdom has been divided and given over to the Medes and Persians."

Then Belshazzar gave orders, and they clothed Daniel with purple and put a necklace of gold around his neck, and issued a proclamation concerning him that he now had authority as the third ruler in the kingdom.

That same night Belshazzar the Chaldean king was slain. So Darius the Mede received the kingdom at about the age of sixty-two (vv. 25-31).

Hearing this interpretation, King Belshazzar went out of his mind and ordered that Daniel should be rewarded. That very night, however, the city of Babylon fell. On the same night Belshazzar blasphemed God, Medo-Persian armies changed the course of the Euphrates River which had passed through the middle of the city. Then, as soon as the river dried up, the enemy invaded it like surging waves.

That night the king was slain, and Babylon fell. When Belshazzar's father, King Nabonidas, heard the news, he rushed with an army to rescue his son. But he too was defeated in battle and became a prisoner. Thus, as Jeremiah and Isaiah had both prophesied, Babylon was destroyed within twenty years.

6

Daniel in the Lions' Den

The False Charge Against Daniel (6:1-9)

*It seemed good to Darius to appoint 120 satraps over
the kingdom, that they should be in charge of the whole
kingdom, and over them three commissioners (of whom
Daniel was one), that these satraps might be accoun-
table to them, and that the king might not suffer loss.
Then this Daniel began distinguishing himself among
the commissioners and satraps because he possessed an
extraordinary spirit, and the king planned to appoint
him over the entire kingdom (vv. 1-3).*

When Daniel was quite old, approaching ninety, he was
once again promoted to the position of administrator—
this time in the kingdom of Darius the Mede. After the conquest of Babylon, King Darius had divided his kingdom into
120 provinces and appointed 120 satraps to rule the provinces,
setting three administrators over them to supervise the collec-
tion of royal revenue. Among the three administrators, Daniel

was most likely the oldest.

Daniel had no worldly desires. He was honest, and as he served the king with such integrity of heart, Darius grew greatly attached to him. Furthermore, though Daniel was old, he was inferior to none in sagacity and excelled in every matter. So the king planned to set him over the whole kingdom. But not everyone was pleased with his plans.

> *Then the commissioners and satraps began trying to find a ground of accusation against Daniel in regard to government affairs; but they could find no ground of accusation or evidence of corruption, inasmuch as he was faithful, and no negligence or corruption was to be found in him. Then these men said, "We shall not find any ground of accusation against this Daniel unless we find it against him with regard to the law of his God"* (vv. 4,5).

The two other administrators were evidently jealous of Daniel. They probably complained that the young people did not have the opportunity to be promoted because of him. Moreover, Daniel was an exile who had been taken captive from Judah, so his prominence and power seemed an insult to native citizens. Consequently, those two administrators conspired together with the satraps against Daniel, and they probably reasoned with them with words like these:

If Daniel becomes the chief administrator, we'll have to serve him. We won't be promoted, and you won't be either. So we must knock him down from the position—but how? Since he doesn't desire worldly gains or political ambition, there's only one way we can bring any charge against this man. We've noticed that he prays to his God three times a day without fail, opening the windows toward Jerusalem. So let's find a way to make this the basis for charges against him.

Then those who had thus conspired hatched a plot.

> *Then these commissioners and satraps came by agree-*
> *ment to the king and spoke to him as follows: "King*
> *Darius, live forever! All the commissioners of the*
> *kingdom, the prefects and the satraps, the high officials*
> *and the governors have consulted together that the king*
> *should establish a statute and enforce an injunction that*
> *anyone who makes a petition to any god or man besides*
> *you, O king, for thirty days, shall be cast into the lions'*
> *den. Now, O king, establish the injunction and sign the*
> *document so that it may not be changed, according to*
> *the law of the Medes and Persians, which may not be*
> *revoked." Therefore King Darius signed the document,*
> *that is, the injunction (vv. 6-9).*

This pleased King Darius, for he thought that he would make the most of this opportunity to unify the empire, establish official discipline and elevate his own authority. So he consented to make it a decree and signed it with his royal ring so that it could not be changed.

The two administrators who had seen this must have danced with joy. They thought they had finally caught Daniel in a trap, and they would soon win the confidence of the king.

Of course, Daniel must have known well about this matter. A candidate for the chief administrator of the kingdom could not have been ignorant of what was happening. He knew exactly what the edict forbade and what punishment it threatened. So how did he respond?

Daniel's Faith Disregarded Peril (6:10-15)

Now when Daniel knew that the document was signed,

81

he entered his house (now in his roof chamber he had windows open toward Jerusalem); and he continued kneeling on his knees three times a day, praying and giving thanks before his God, as he had been doing previously. Then these men came by agreement and found Daniel making petition and supplication before his God (v. 10,11).

Despite the threat of death, Daniel went home, opened the window toward Jerusalem and prayed on his knees three times a day as usual. We should not be surprised, for even his enemies had been certain that he would still pray, however severe and strict the royal decree might be.

If Daniel had departed just a little from his convictions, he could have avoided danger. He did not have to open the windows in full public view while he prayed, for God is not bound by any such external condition. If he had prayed clandestinely after the others went to bed instead of insisting on his custom of praying three times at a set hour, he could not have been charged with disobeying the law. But Daniel would not compromise even a little. Consequently, he was accused.

Then they approached and spoke before the king about the king's injunction, "Did you not sign an injunction that any man who makes a petition to any god or man besides you, O king, for thirty days, is to be cast into the lions' den?" The king answered and said, "The statement is true, according to the law of the Medes and Persians, which may not be revoked." Then they answered and spoke before the king, "Daniel, who is one of the exiles from Judah, pays no attention to you, O king, or to the injunction which you signed, but keeps making his petition three times a day" (vv. 12,13).

The administrators knew that the king could not change the law without subverting his own authority and his nation's traditions. So they had him trapped into passing the death sentence on Daniel.

Then, as soon as the king heard this statement, he was deeply distressed and set his mind on delivering Daniel; and even until sunset he kept exerting himself to rescue him. Then these men came by agreement to the king and said to the king, "Recognize, O king, that it is a law of the Medes and Persians that no injunction or statute which the king establishes may be changed" (vv. 14,15).

The king realized belatedly that an evil scheme lay behind the decree, and he was deeply distressed. Now we must keep in mind that in those days it was considered a matter of little consequence for a king, who typically put little value on human life, to throw a lawbreaker into the lions' den. Yet King Darius was distressed. Evidently Daniel's loyalty to Darius and the firmness of his faith in God were so great that the king was deeply impressed and moved.

So Darius determined to rescue Daniel and made every effort until sundown to save him. He probably analyzed the decree closely in the hope of finding some clause by which he might possibly rescue the old man. When Darius delayed, however, the accusers came again to the king in a group and pressed him with a reminder that the law of the Medes and Persians could not be changed. They were implying that if the king did not carry out the decree he had issued, he would have difficulty in ruling over the kingdom. In this way the king found himself bound by the decree he had issued even though he was absolute in power; and because of his faith in God, Daniel was put to the test.

Daniel's Test of Faith (6:16-18)

Then the king gave orders, and Daniel was brought in and cast into the lions' den. The king spoke and said to Daniel, "Your God whom you constantly serve will Himself deliver you." And a stone was brought and laid over the mouth of the den; and the king sealed it with his own signet ring and with the signet rings of his nobles, so that nothing might be changed in regard to Daniel. Then the king went off to his palace and spent the night fasting, and no entertainment was brought before him; and his sleep fled from him.

Notice here the love of Darius toward Daniel. Even a heathen king who was ignorant of God was so deeply moved by the integrity of Daniel's character and the firmness of his faith in God that he made a confession of faith before Daniel. In essence, he said: "Daniel, though I have tried hard all day long to deliver you, it's beyond my power to deliver you. But I'm sure that your God will deliver you from the lions' den."

Our own proclamation of Jesus through our life of faith should bear fruit like this. Daniel, who had made King Nebuchadnezzar of Babylon surrender himself to God, now changed King Darius of the Medes and Persians as well.

Listen to the king's confession of positive faith. We should also have this faith which Daniel possessed so that others will believe in our God and confess faith along with us.

When the king had given his orders against his will, the two administrators and the 120 satraps were perhaps afraid that the king might change his heart and rescue Daniel. So after Daniel was thrown in the lions' den they had a stone placed at the mouth of the den and sealed with the royal signet ring, adding the seals of the nobles as well. Finally they could rest easy, thinking that the matter was over. Surely, they said, the lions would tear old Daniel to pieces.

How distressed King Darius was after he had ordered Daniel's death! He spent the night restlessly, while a still and solemn atmosphere hung low around the whole palace.

God's Protection (6:19-23)

Then the king arose with the dawn, at the break of day, and went in haste to the lions' den. And when he had come near the den to Daniel, he cried out with a troubled voice. The king spoke and said to Daniel, "Daniel, servant of the living God, has your God, whom you constantly serve, been able to deliver you from the lions?" Then Daniel spoke to the king, "O king, live forever! My God sent His angel and shut the lions' mouths, and they have not harmed me, inasmuch as I was found innocent before Him; and also toward you, O king, I have committed no crime." Then the king was very pleased and gave orders for Daniel to be taken up out of the den. So Daniel was taken up out of the den, and no injury whatever was found on him, because he had trusted in his God.

At the first light of dawn, the king arose and hurried to the lions' den. Though he hoped on one hand that the God of Daniel had surely delivered him, his question showed that he could not quite believe it. But Daniel's response dispelled his doubt.

Notice how even in the lions' den Daniel maintained the courtesy which he had always shown in the presence of the king. Evidently, he had spent the previous night with a calmness of heart—which is more than we can say for the king.

Daniel's words—"My God sent His angel and shut the lions'

mouths''—were echoed centuries later by another man of great faith, the apostle Paul. When Paul was sailing for Italy, the ship he was on was overtaken by a storm and drifted for two weeks. But while others feared, Paul declared: ''And yet now I urge you to keep up your courage, for there shall be no loss of life among you, but only of the ship. For this very night an angel of the God to whom I belong and whom I serve stood before me...'' (Acts 27:22,23).

Not only in the time of Daniel and the apostle Paul, but in our time as well, God sends His angel to deliver those who trust in Him and serve Him with sincere hearts. As God shut the mouths of the lions, quenched the power of fire in the furnace, and stilled the raging storms in the sea, He can protect us from all kinds of trials.

Today as in Daniel's day, the angels of the Lord are the messengers sent by God to protect and serve the heirs of God who are saved. If our eyes were opened and were able to see the spiritual world, we could see the angels standing around us; for wherever the people of God gather together, the angels of the Lord always surround them.

Judgment Against Daniel's Enemies (6:24)

The king then gave orders, and they brought those men who had maliciously accused Daniel, and they cast them, their children, and their wives into the lions' den; and they had not reached the bottom of the den before the lions overpowered them and crushed all their bones.

The lions must have been very hungry because the angel had kept them from eating all night. How ferociously those lions must have leaped upon Daniel's enemies when the king had them thrown in the den instead!

Notice here: Those who do not believe in Jesus may lay a snare for Christians, but they always get themselves ensnared instead. Who would have thought that the schemers themselves would be thrown into the lions' den that had been prepared for Daniel? Or think of what happened in the book of Esther. Who would have thought that Haman would be hanged on the gallows which he himself had prepared for Mordecai?

Remembering this, those who believe in the Lord, trusting in Him, will have nothing to fear. If we keep the integrity of our faith, even though we walk through the valley of the shadow of death, the rod and staff of the Lord will comfort us, and He will prepare a table for us in the presence of our enemies (see Ps. 23). Since God is with us, who can be against us?

The Faith of King Darius (6:25-28)

Then Darius the king wrote to all the peoples, nations, and men of every language who were living in all the land: "May your peace abound! I make a decree that in all the dominion of my kingdom men are to fear and tremble before the God of Daniel;

For He is the living God and enduring forever,
And His kingdom is one which will not be destroyed,
And His dominion will be forever.
He delivers and rescues and performs signs and wonders
In heaven and on earth,
Who has also delivered Daniel from the power of the lions."
So this Daniel enjoyed success in the reign of Darius and in the reign of Cyrus the Persian.

Daniel's deliverance from the lions' den was so impressive

that King Darius wrote immediately a decree to all the people throughout the empire. This decree was a wonderful confession of faith, just as the earlier decree of King Nebuchadnezzar of Babylon had been. God is not only the God of Judah and Israel, but also the God who controls the history of all human beings.

King Darius did not see God, but he did see the God of Daniel. In the time of Nebuchadnezzar, the king did not see God either, but he did see the God of Shadrach, Meshach and Abednego.

The same is true today. Many people don't know about God, but they do know about your God. They picture God in their minds through your words and behavior. So just as King Darius called God the God of Daniel, you should live in such a way that others will call God your God. Let them see your God in such a way that they confess, "We must fear this person's God."

Even though Babylon conquered Judah, carrying many of its people as captives to their land, Babylon's kings and kingdoms knelt down before the God of their captives and surrendered to Him. In the same way, our spiritual faith still has greater power than the atomic bombs or the hydrogen bombs of the world. We serve the God of Daniel.

Korea is perhaps located disadvantageously from a geopolitical standpoint; but as long as Korea serves the God of Daniel, the Lord God almighty who is with us, we have nothing to fear. The God of Shadrach, Meshach and Abednego, the God of Daniel and the God of the apostle Paul is our God and is with us all. No lion will open its mouth to devour us.

> If God is for us, who is against us? He who did not spare his own Son, but delivered Him up for us all, how will He not also with Him freely give us all things? Who

will bring a charge against God's elect? God is the one who justifies; who is the one who condemns? Christ Jesus is He who died, yes, rather who was raised, who is at the right hand of God, who also intercedes for us. Who shall separate us from the love of Christ? Shall tribulation, or distress, or persecution, or famine, or nakedness, or peril, or sword? (Rom. 8:31-35).

7

Daniel's Vision of the Four Beasts

The Four Winds of Heaven (7:1,2)

In the first year of Belshazzar king of Babylon Daniel saw a dream and visions in his mind as he lay on his bed; then he wrote the dream down and related the following summary of it. Daniel said, "I was looking in my vision by night, and behold, the four winds of heaven were stirring up the great sea."

Daniel chapter 7 deals with the revelation Daniel received in a dream in the first year of Belshazzar, king of Babylon, which was fourteen years before Babylon fell. Daniel saw first in this dream the four winds of heaven churning up the great sea. The winds of heaven signified the providence of God and God's sovereignty over human history. That the winds came from heaven meant that human history goes on within the boundaries of the divine will. In other words, whatever rebellion the devil may raise, it cannot make any change in the course of human history that God has not allowed.

"The great sea" in the Bible always refers to the Mediterranean. So the phrase "the four winds of the heaven were stirring up the great sea" set the scene for a forecast of historic events that by the providence of God would unfold in the countries surrounding the Mediterranean Sea.

The Lion With the Wings of an Eagle (7:3,4)

"And four great beasts were coming up from the sea, different from one another.
"The first was like a lion and had the wings of an eagle. I kept looking until its wings were plucked, and it was lifted up from the ground and made to stand on two feet like a man; a human mind also was given to it."

The first beast which came up from the sea, a lion with eagle's wings, referred to Babylon. It corresponded to the golden head of the statue King Nebuchadnezzar had seen in his dream.

Why was Babylon represented as a lion with eagle's wings? Sculptures of such a creature stood before the gate of the Babylonian palace. An eagle is king among the birds of the air, while a lion is king among the animals on the earth. So this creature reflected the absolute power of the Babylonian monarch and the perfect organization of Babylonian bureaucracy. It also meant that Babylon would conquer all the known world of the day with the swiftness and power of an eagle's wings, becoming a mighty power.

While Daniel watched the lion, its wings were torn off, and it was lifted from the ground so that it stood on two feet like a human being. This referred to the mysterious incident which had happened to King Nebuchadnezzar when his arrogance caused him to be judged by God with insanity for seven years.

That the eagle's wings were torn off means that power

departed from King Nebuchadnezzar. Yet when he recovered, he did not become like an animal but rather like a human being.

In this vision, God depicted each kingdom and the king of the world through the image of a beast. But when Nebuchadnezzar deeply repented of his folly, acknowledging the divine sovereignty, God made him stand up like a human being. Nebuchadnezzar, who repented before God, became a beautiful person in God's sight. Thus the first beast Daniel saw referred to his own age, the age of Babylon.

The Bear With Three Ribs Between Its Teeth (7:5)

"And behold, another beast, a second one, resembling a bear. And it was raised up on one side, and three ribs were in its mouth between its teeth; and thus they said to it, 'Arise, devour much meat!' "

Daniel saw this vision during the reign of Belshazzar, the last king of Babylon. The second beast in the vision, a bear, revealed the age which was to come next. It represented the kingdom of the Medes and Persians, which was to rise through the conquest of Babylon and last about two centuries, to 331 B.C.

Like a bear, the Medes and Persians were stupid and tactless but strong. When they waged a war, they needed little strategy; they just pushed with the power of the sheer numbers in their enormous army, which ranged from a hundred thousand up to a million. The number they mobilized in their campaign against the Greeks amounted to a million, with one half of the army as a regular battle force and the other half as supporting groups.

The Medo-Persian empire was not only stupid and tactless, but also cruel. It conquered many countries, trampling them under their feet.

The bear in the vision was raised up on its side. This showed that, although the Medes and Persians were a coalition of two kingdoms, the empire leaned to one side, the side of Persia; for Persia, which was built later than Media, came to supremacy and eventually defeated the Medes. The silver breast and arms beneath the golden head in Nebuchadnezzar's dream also corresponded to this coalition of the Medes and Persians.

In the vision the bear had three ribs between its teeth. These three ribs signified the strong nations conquered by the Medo-Persian empire: Babylon, Lydia and Egypt. The voice which said, "Devour much flesh," represented the divine grant given to the Medo-Persian empire to have dominion over many neighboring countries. According to that divine grant, the Medes and Persians conquered many small nations in the Near East, expanding their territory far greater than the territory Babylon had once possessed. This lasted for more than two centuries, but the empire finally fell, and the third beast appeared.

The Leopard With Four Wings and Four Heads (7:6)

"After this I kept looking, and behold, another one, like a leopard, which had on its back four wings of a bird; the beast also had four heads, and dominion was given to it."

Imagine this beast. A leopard is a fast animal, and this leopard had four wings on its back. What could be faster than a flying leopard?

This creature referred to Alexander the Great, the Greek general who conquered Medo-Persia and gained control of much of the world. He was the greatest conqueror the world had ever seen, occupying a vast territory in a short time. Alexander rose from Macedonia in Europe and conquered large portions of Asia and Africa, sweeping like a storm all the way to the borders of India.

Legend has it that Alexander wept, sitting at the bank of the Indus River, because there was no more land to conquer. But soon after that he died of a fever in Babylon at the age of thirty-three.

The four heads of this leopard referred to the four generals of Alexander the Great; that is, the collective leadership system of his empire. In Alexander's conquest of the world his four generals played a central role, and after Alexander's death they divided the entire Greek kingdom among themselves. Thrace and Bithynia went to the first general, Lysimachus; Macedonia and Greece to the second, Cassander; Syria and Babylon to the third, Seleucus; and Egypt, Palestine and Arabia to the fourth, Ptolemy. In this way Alexander's empire was divided into four kingdoms that constantly warred against each other.

The Beast With Ten Horns (7:7,8)

"After this I kept looking in the night visions, and behold, a fourth beast, dreadful and terrifying and extremely strong; and it had large iron teeth. It devoured and crushed, and trampled down the remainder with its feet; and it was different from all the beasts that were before it, and it had ten horns. While I was contemplating the horns, behold, another horn, a little one, came up among them, and three of the first horns were pulled out by the roots before it; and behold, this horn possessed eyes like the eyes of a man, and a mouth uttering great boasts."

The fourth beast Daniel saw was terrifying and powerful.

It had large iron teeth and ten horns. This beast referred to the Roman empire, which succeeded Greece and brought the whole world under its sway.

The city of Rome, which began as a small village on the River Tiber in Italy, began to extend its territory through wars with its neighbors in the fourth century B.C. By the turn of the second century B.C., it had already conquered Spain and Carthage. Then it continued to further its conquests, adding Macedonia, Greece and Asia Minor to its dominions. Eventually Syria and Jerusalem fell to Rome, as well as the European lands which today are home to Great Britain, France, Belgium, Switzerland and Germany.

By the early years of the second century A.D., the Roman empire was at the height of its prosperity. Its vast territory included almost all of Europe, and its power even reached to the border of India. Thus Rome succeeded in building the largest empire in human history. Yet even Rome fell to invading armies in A.D. 410. No human kingdom lasts forever.

In Daniel's vision, this terrifying fourth beast crushed and devoured its victims and trampled underfoot what was left. This showed that Rome, driven by the lust for conquest, would relentlessly pursue a policy of expansionism, crushing the subjugated countries. In fact, the massacre of subjugated people took place frequently in the Roman empire, with thousands of people often killed at one time. Those who survived the massacres, hundreds of thousands of them, were carried off as prisoners of war and sold as slaves. Thus in the wake of the Roman armies, civilization was often reduced to ashes.

As we noted before, the period of two thousand years which followed the age of Rome does not appear in Jewish prophecy. Jesus came to this world in the age of Rome, and the two thousand years which come between that time and the second coming of Jesus are the age of the gospel, the period in which all humankind can be delivered by the cross of Jesus Christ. This period has nothing to do with Judaism, so God did not show it to the prophets of the Old Testament.

When the two thousand years of the church age come to a close at the end of the world, then, according to Daniel's vision, ten horns will suddenly come up from the head of the terrifying beast which is Rome. Next a little horn will come up among the ten horns, uprooting three of them. In the vision this horn had human eyes and a mouth that spoke boastfully.

This part of the vision paralleled Nebuchadnezzar's dream in that it showed that at the end of the world ten kingdoms will be unified in the former territory of Rome. Twenty-six hundred years ago, Daniel prophesied accurately the historic fact that ten kingdoms would arise from the former territory of Rome.

The little horn, which came up among ten horns, referred to the antichrist. This antichrist will arise and oppose God, toppling three kingdoms and unifying the remaining seven. All these things are elaborated upon in Revelation 13.

As we noted before in chapter 2, the last part of this world's history will begin with the unification of the ten kingdoms of Europe, Rome's former territory—and that unification is underway right now. Daniel saw this in his vision twenty-six hundred years ago, but he did not know then what it meant. We, however, are living in the very age of that prophecy, so we can observe with our own eyes how ten kingdoms arising in Europe are coming together in the European Economic Community.

When ten countries in this former territory of Rome are thus unified politically, economically and militarily, a supreme leader will arise from it and will conquer three countries out of ten.

After that he will subdue the remaining seven countries, bringing all of Europe under his feet. He will dictate to the world, speaking boastfully to God. Then, as we can see from a study of Revelation, he will launch a campaign against the Jews.

As we have also noted before in chapter 2, around the time when the unification of ten countries is completed in Europe, we Christians will be taken up into heaven all at once. That is why we should pray all the more to receive the fullness of the Holy Spirit as the time draws near. We do not know when the unification will be completed. Some think the European Community that will be established in 1992 will be the fulfillment of these prophecies. Others believe it is only the beginning of the process that will lead to full political unification.

These political trends indicate that the second coming of Christ is imminent.

The Judgment Against the Antichrist (7:9-12)

"I kept looking
Until thrones were set up,
And the Ancient of Days took His seat;
His vesture was like white snow,
And the hair of His head like pure wool.
His throne was ablaze with flames,
Its wheels were a burning fire.
A river of fire was flowing
And coming out from before Him;
Thousands upon thousands were attending Him,
And myriads upon myriads were standing before Him;
The court sat,
And the books were opened.
"Then I kept looking because of the sound of the
boastful words which the horn was speaking; I kept

looking until the beast was slain, and its body was destroyed and given to the burning fire. As for the rest of the beasts, their dominion was taken away, but an extension of life was granted to them for an appointed period of time."

As soon as the era of ten horns passed in the vision, the judgment against the little horn, the antichrist, approached. At this time Daniel saw the judgment seat of God, the Ancient of Days, set in place. Those who attended Him were angels and those who stood before Him were the bride of Jesus Christ—that is, the saints who had been resurrected and had gone to heaven.

The Bible further says that in Daniel's vision the court was seated, and the books were opened. This judgment signifies the one that will take place shortly after the tribulation Jesus prophesied (see Matt. 24:21). From the moment the antichrist completes the unification of Europe, the tribulation will begin, and the antichrist will reign for seven years.

According to my interpretation of this passage and the book of Revelation, following the tribulation, Christ and His faithful saints will descend from heaven, and right after the battle of Armageddon, Christ will take captive the antichrist and his false prophets. After judging them, He will cast them into the lake burning with fire and brimstone.

This judgment against the antichrist which Daniel saw twenty-six hundred years ago is also mentioned in Revelation 19. During that period any individual or nation with the mark of the beast will also be judged. But there is a particular order in the events of the judgment according to John's vision in Revelation chapters 19 and 20.

First, the antichrist and his false prophets will be taken and cast into the lake burning with fire and brimstone.

Second, the other beasts of the ten kingdoms will be stripped of their authority but allowed to live for a period of time until the kingdom of one thousand years begins (Dan. 7:12). Then they will be judged and cast into hell, where they will remain for a thousand years.

Third, after that thousand years, the judgment of the great white throne of God begins. At this time all the dead will rise to be judged finally, and they will be cast into the lake burning with fire and brimstone.

The Everlasting Kingdom of Christ (7:13,14)

"I kept looking in the night visions,
And behold, with the clouds of heaven
One like a Son of Man was coming,
And He came up to the Ancient of Days
And was presented before Him.
And to Him was given dominion,
Glory and a kingdom,
That all the peoples, nations, and men of every
language
Might serve Him.
His dominion is an everlasting dominion
Which will not pass away;
And His kingdom is one
Which will not be destroyed."

While Jesus was in this world, He frequently called Himself the Son of Man. Here Daniel says, "With the clouds of heaven, one like a Son of Man was coming." The "one like a Son of Man" whom Daniel saw in the night visions was Jesus Christ Himself.

The clouds of heaven represent not only glory but also the crowds. Accordingly, in this scene Jesus comes down from heaven not only in glory but accompanied by His bride, the multitude of His saints. This event takes place after the judgment in which Jesus Christ takes over the thousand-year kingdom from His Father.

Some day we will be with God and will be His heirs. The Bible says it this way: "The Spirit Himself bears witness with our spirit that we are children of God, and if children, heirs also, heirs of God and fellow-heirs with Christ, if indeed we suffer with Him in order that we may also be glorified with Him" (Rom. 8:16-17).

The dominion which we inherit as fellow-heirs with Christ will be eternal and His kingdom will be an everlasting kingdom. I pray in the Lord Jesus' name that none of you lose the blessing of inheriting this dominion and kingdom.

The Interpretation of the Fourth Kingdom (7:15-28)

"As for me, Daniel, my spirit was distressed within me, and the visions in my mind kept alarming me. I approached one of those who were standing by and began asking him the exact meaning of all this. So he told me and made known to me the interpretation of these things..." (vv. 15,16).

The vision of the fourth kingdom troubled Daniel's heart because he didn't know what it meant. He had been able to interpret the meaning of the other beasts, but this one was quite different. So he approached the angel who had brought him the vision and asked its meaning.

" 'These great beasts, which are four in number, are four kings who will arise from the earth. But the saints of the Highest One will receive the kingdom and possess the kingdom forever, for all ages to come.' Then I

101

desired to know the exact meaning of the fourth beast, which was different from all the others, exceedingly dreadful, with its teeth of iron and its claws of bronze, and which devoured, crushed, and trampled down the remainder with its feet, and the meaning of the ten horns that were on its head, and the other horn which came up, and before which three of them fell, namely, that horn which had eyes and a mouth uttering great boasts, and which was larger in appearance than its associates" (vv. 17-20).

Though Daniel had trouble understanding, the beast is not beyond our understanding because we have already studied about it. It is obvious from the angel's explanation of the vision that the fourth kingdom refers to Rome; the ten horns signify the ten kingdoms which will rise in the former territory of Rome at the end of the world; and the little horn signifies the antichrist. According to that explanation, the antichrist will first unify the three kingdoms, then he will expand his dominion over the other seven kingdoms.

"I kept looking, and that horn was waging war with the saints and overpowering them until the Ancient of Days came, and judgment was passed in favor of the saints of the Highest One, and the time arrived when the saints took possession of the kingdom.

"Thus he said: 'The fourth beast will be a fourth kingdom on the earth, which will be different from all the other kingdoms, and it will devour the whole earth and tread it down and crush it. As for the ten horns, out of this kingdom ten kings will arise; and another will arise after them, and he will be different from the previous ones and will subdue three kings' " (vv. 21-24).

Then the antichrist will wage war against the saints of God. Here "the saints" refers to two groups: the Jews and the Christians who were not prepared when Jesus descended from heaven. Those Spirit-filled Christians who had prepared themselves and waited for the coming of Jesus had been already taken up into heaven around the time of the antichrist's appearance.

> " *'And he will speak out against the Most High and wear down the saints of the Highest One, and he will intend to make alterations in times and in law; and they will be given into his hand for a time, times, and half a time. But the court will sit for judgment, and his dominion will be taken away, annihilated and destroyed forever. Then the sovereignty, the dominion, and the greatness of all the kingdoms under the whole heaven will be given to the people of the saints of the Highest One; His kingdom will be an everlasting kingdom, and all the dominions will serve and obey Him.' At this point the revelation ended. As for me, Daniel, my thoughts were greatly alarming me and my face grew pale, but I kept the matter to myself"* (vv. 25-28).

According to Daniel, the antichrist will try to change the set times and the laws. He will dislike the present name of our era, A.D. or "Anno Domini," which means "the year of the Lord." Thus he will loathe to hear words like "A.D. 1999," because it means "the year of the Lord 1999," a year in the era whose beginning is Jesus Christ. He will also change laws in order to place himself at the center of law, and he will institute a new era.

From this time on, the Jewish people will be delivered into the hand of the antichrist for "a time, times and half a time" (7:25), and they will go through the tribulation. This is dealt with in detail in Revelation 11. During the first three and a half years of the tribulation there will be natural disasters. During the second three and a half years the antichrist will set up his own idol in the temple of God in violation of the seven-year treaty which he had previously agreed upon with the Jews. Then he will launch a dreadful campaign against the Jews.

But verse 22 says that the Ancient of Days—that is, God— came and pronounced judgment in favor of the saints. The antichrist was taken and destroyed. All the world became the kingdom of Christ, and it was given to the saints. This will happen at the last judgment.

For us the book of Daniel is no longer a sealed book (see 12:4), but an open book. What Daniel could not understand, we can now see clearly. Nevertheless, the devil is furious that we know in advance, through the study of these books and prayer, the things that will happen in the future. That is why many pastors hesitate to examine the book of Daniel. They are afraid of being attacked by the devil in spirit or in body. Even so, every believing saint can clearly know the contents of the book now that history has opened up what was sealed.

Today you and I live in this wonderful age believing in Jesus. Is there anything for which we could be more grateful?

8

A Ram and a Goat

The Secret of a Ram With Two Horns (8:1-4)

In the third year of the reign of Belshazzar the king a vision appeared to me, Daniel, subsequent to the one which appeared to me previously. And I looked in the vision, and it came about while I was looking, that I was in the citadel of Susa, which is in the province of Elam; and I looked in the vision, and I myself was beside the Ulai Canal. Then I lifted my gaze and looked, and behold, a ram which had two horns was standing in front of the canal. Now the two horns were long, but one was longer than the other, with the longer one coming up last. I saw the ram butting westward, northward, and southward, and no other beasts could stand before him, nor was there anyone to rescue from his power; but he did as he pleased and magnified himself.

The ram with two horns signifies the Medo-Persian empire. Strange as it may sound, the kings of the Medo-Persian

105

empire wore helmets which looked like rams' horns, instead of a crown, when they went into battle. Accordingly, this prophecy accurately depicts the Medo-Persian kings going to war.

Referring to the Medo-Persian empire, Daniel's vision showed the horn which grew up later as becoming longer than the first. This revealed that even though Media came to power earlier than Persia, it was conquered by Persia, which by annexing it built a united empire.

The Medo-Persian empire was located in the East between Egypt and Asia. It expanded its territory by conquering Greece westward, Babylon northward and Egypt southward. This was prophesied in verse 4.

The Goat From the West (8:5-8)

While I was observing, behold, a male goat was coming from the west over the surface of the whole earth without touching the ground; and the goat had a conspicuous horn between his eyes. And he came up to the ram that had the two horns, which I had seen standing in front of the canal, and rushed at him in his mighty wrath. And I saw him come beside the ram, and he was enraged at him; and he struck the ram and shattered his two horns, and the ram had no strength to withstand him. So he hurled him to the ground and trampled on him, and there was none to rescue the ram from his power. Then the male goat magnified himself exceedingly. But as soon as he was mighty, the large horn was broken; and in its place there came up four conspicuous horns toward the four winds of heaven.

When the ram with two horns increased greatly, charging toward the west, the north and the south, suddenly a goat came running. This goat refers to the Greek empire, and the horn between the eyes signifies Alexander the Great, whom we have mentioned before.

Before this king's conquest of the Medo-Persian empire, the Greeks had themselves been invaded by the Persians, who had waged a campaign with a great army that was one million strong. Since then, Greece had waited bitterly for revenge. Finally the opportunity arrived. When he was only thirty, Alexander, the son of King Philip of Macedonia, led a sizeable army on an expedition against the Medo-Persian empire. Yet compared to the vast army of the Medo-Persians, the Greeks were numerically inferior.

Daniel said that the goat was so strong and fast it ran even without touching the ground. That is how Alexander's army swiftly advanced and defeated the large army of Persia at the Granicus River of Asia Minor in May 334 B.C.

A year and a half later, in November 333 B.C., Persia again raised an army and fought with Greece at Issus by the northern tip of the Mediterranean Sea. His troops were smashed by Alexander. Then in October 331 B.C., two years later, Greece and Persia had a final showdown at Gaugamela near Nineveh, where Alexander trampled Persia once and for all.

Thus the ram, which stood for Persia, was completely conquered by the goat, which stood for Greece. Then the vision further showed that the large horn of this goat was broken off, and in its place four prominent horns grew up toward the four winds of heaven. This showed that Alexander would die young and that his empire would be divided into four parts by his four generals, as we saw in chapter 7.

A Little Horn (8:9-12)

And out of one of them came forth a rather small horn

which grew exceedingly great toward the south, toward the east, and toward the Beautiful Land. And it grew up to the host of heaven and caused some of the host and some of the stars to fall to the earth, and it trampled them down. It even magnified itself to be equal with the Commander of the host; and it removed the regular sacrifice from Him, and the place of His sanctuary was thrown down. And on account of transgression the host will be given over to the horn along with the regular sacrifice; and it will fling truth to the ground and perform its will and prosper.

Now we have a story about a little horn which is quite mysterious and difficult to understand. This little horn is different from the one which appeared in chapter 7. This second prophecy of a little horn was already fulfilled historically, but at the same time it stands for the antichrist which is yet to come.

After the world was divided by the four generals of Alexander the Great, two of the four resulting kingdoms eventually emerged as major forces: Syria, taken by Seleucus, and Egypt, taken by Ptolemy. These two kingdoms were constantly engaged in hostile actions.

Israel was sandwiched geographically between the two kingdoms. When Egypt came up to fight Syria, Israel was trampled underfoot. When Syria went down to fight Egypt, Israel was also stamped down. Thus the sufferings of Israel were beyond description.

Under these circumstances, according to Daniel, a little horn came up out of one of the horns. The description that follows in Daniel's account fits perfectly a king of Syria named Antiochus Epiphanes, who was eighth in the Seleucus dynasty (175-164 B.C.).

Antiochus rose to prominence among the four horns. He

defeated Egypt, and on his way home, he subdued Jerusalem. After Jerusalem surrendered, he set himself up against God and cruelly trampled Israel underfoot. "The host" in Daniel's vision refers to the Jews whom this conqueror cast down in defeat.

Antiochus murdered several of the political and religious leaders of Israel, including the high priest Onias III, the religious star of the Jews in that day. Moreover, he set himself up to be as great as the Prince of the host—that is, God. He forbade the daily sacrifice in the temple. He desecrated the sanctuary with an altar offered to the Greek deity he worshipped. On it he sacrificed swine's blood, an abomination to the Jews. No worse sacrilege could be imagined.

Yet he went further. He abolished the Mosaic law, which was held to be most sacred by the Jews. He forbade circumcision and imposed a pagan life-style upon them. And anyone who refused to obey Antiochus or rebelled against him was subject to death.

These events parallel what will come to pass in the last days: the rise of the antichrist in the tribulation and his conquest and cruel treatment of Israel. The tragedy that already happened once in the history of Israel will be repeated in the future by the antichrist.

In that day, the antichrist will break down the altar in the sanctuary, setting up in its place his own idol. He will force the Jews to worship the idol and will take away the daily sacrifice which is offered morning and evening. And he will abolish the law of Moses, imposing a pagan life-style on the Jews.

The Blasphemy of the Little Horn (8:13,14)

Then I heard a holy one speaking, and another holy one said to that particular one who was speaking, "How

long will the vision about the regular sacrifice apply,
while the transgression causes horror, so as to allow
both the holy place and the host to be trampled?'' And
he said to me, ''For 2,300 evenings and mornings; then
the holy place will be properly restored.''

These words of the angels came true in history. The persecution against the Jews began in 171 B.C. and continued until Antiochus finally died on an expedition to Media in 164 B.C. As soon as he died, Israel was released from Syrian bondage. The temple was purged, and the daily sacrifice was restored. The number of days from Antiochus's conquest of Israel to his death was exactly twenty-three hundred, the number prophesied here.

Because this is a double prophecy which was once fulfilled in history yet will be fulfilled again at the end of the world, this passage shows clearly that some day the antichrist, like Antiochus Epiphanes, will arise to destroy Israel and to desecrate the sanctuary. As we have already seen, that period will be "a time, times, and half a time" (7:25).

Gabriel's Interpretation of the Vision (8:15-27)

And it came about when I, Daniel, had seen the vision,
that I sought to understand it; and behold, standing
before me was one who looked like a man. And I heard
the voice of a man between the banks of Ulai, and he
called out and said, ''Gabriel, give this man an under-
standing of the vision'' (vv. 15,16).

When Daniel saw this vision he was distressed because he could not understand it. But then he heard a man's voice from the opposite side of the river commanding Gabriel to explain it. As an archangel heralding divine messages, Gabriel was one of the highest among the angels, along with Michael, who was captain of the heavenly host. So this must have been the voice of Jesus, for no one but He had the authority to give orders to Gabriel.

> *So he came near to where I was standing, and when he came I was frightened and fell on my face; but he said to me, "Son of man, understand that the vision pertains to the time of the end." Now while he was talking with me, I sank into a deep sleep with my face to the ground; but he touched me and made me stand upright. And he said, "Behold, I am going to let you know what will occur at the final period of the indignation, for it pertains to the appointed time of the end. The ram which you saw with the two horns represents the kings of Media and Persia. And the shaggy goat represents the kingdom of Greece, and the large horn that is between his eyes is the first king. And the broken horn and the four horns that arose in its place represent four kingdoms which will arise from his nation, although not with his power"* (vv. 17-22).

Here Gabriel explained the significance of the vision according to the historical outline we have already presented. Then he went on to say that at the latter part of the period of the four kingdoms arising out of Alexander's kingdom would arise a fierce enemy of the Jews. This was Antiochus Epiphanes, but because he was a type of the antichrist, what is said here about him can also be applied to the antichrist who is to come.

A Description of the Antichrist

"And in the latter period of their rule,
When the transgressors have run their course,

A king will arise
Insolent and skilled in intrigue.
And his power will be mighty, but not by his own
  power,
And he will destroy to an extraordinary degree
And prosper and perform his will;
He will destroy mighty men and the holy people.
And through his shrewdness
He will cause deceit to succeed by his influence;
And he will magnify himself in his heart,
And he will destroy many while they are at ease.
He will even oppose the Prince of princes,
But he will be broken without human agency"
  (vv. 23-25).

We are told here first of all that the countenance of the antichrist will be stern. So the president of United Europe prophesied here will be a hard man, hard enough to control all of Europe and to sway the world.

The angel goes on to say that he will be a master of intrigue. This shows that he will manipulate the ten countries of Europe as he wishes because of his great political ability.

The Bible also says here that the antichrist will become very strong, but not by his own power. This aspect is explained by Revelation 13, which tells us that the dragon who is the prince of the air—that is, Satan—will flee away from Michael the archangel. When he comes down to earth, he will enter into the antichrist. Then the antichrist will immediately turn into the beast and, receiving extraordinary ability and supernatural power from Satan, will grip all of Europe in his hands.

As we have previously noted, the antichrist, who has thus achieved the unification of Europe, will enter into a seven-year treaty with Israel. He will help Israel rebuild the temple, which was destroyed by the Romans, at the top of Mount Moriah. He will take advantage of Israel, using the nation for his own purposes for three and a half years until he has enough political power to stand by himself.

Then the antichrist will suddenly turn into the beast, claiming that he is a god. Having his own idol built in the sanctuary, he will force the people to worship it. But monotheistic Israel will never obey that command. Consequently, this will lead to the campaign against the Jews during the latter half of the tribulation.

Referring to this time, Jesus said:

> *"Therefore when you see the abomination of desolation which was spoken of through Daniel the prophet, standing in the holy place (let the reader understand), then let those who are in Judea flee to the mountains; let him who is on the housetop not go down to get the things out that are in his house; and let him who is in the field not turn back to get his cloak. But woe to those who are with child and to those who nurse babes in those days! But pray that your flight may not be in the winter, or on a Sabbath; for then there will be a great tribulation, such as has not occurred since the beginning of the world until now, nor ever shall. And unless those days had been cut short, no life would have been saved; but for the sake of the elect those days shall be cut short"* (Matt. 24:15-22).

Thus the antichrist will persecute the Jews, opposing God and claiming that he is Christ for the second half of the tribulation. Yet the time will come when he will be broken, but not by human power.

The Battle of Armageddon

When will this antichrist fall? During the war of Armageddon (see Rev. 16:16). A vast army will come from the east, mainly from China, and the army of the antichrist will move from Europe to fight with them. Thus there will be a bloody war in Israel.

Nuclear bombs will be used, and blood will flow like a river. At that very moment, Christ will come with His saints. Then the army of the antichrist and the eastern army which has come from China and other Asian countries will stop fighting and will compromise to fight against Christ in concert. But the antichrist will be taken and his entire army will be destroyed by the sharp swords which come out of the mouth of Jesus Christ. Finally, the antichrist, who has been taken by the hand of Christ, will be thrown alive into the lake of fire burning with brimstone, along with his false prophets.

The End of the Age

"And the vision of the evenings and mornings
Which has been told is true;
But keep the vision secret,
For it pertains to many days in the future."
Then I, Daniel, was exhausted and sick for days. Then
I got up again and carried on the king's business; but
I was astounded at the vision, and there was none to
explain it (vv. 26-27).

When Gabriel told Daniel to "keep the vision secret, for it pertains to many days in the future" (v. 26), he meant that, since the things of this vision did not concern Daniel's own age, he had to keep this vision to himself. Meanwhile, the vision was so shocking that after Daniel saw it he lay ill for several days.

Today the vision is no longer secret. We are now at the threshold of the end times. Before long the grace-filled gospel age of Jesus Christ will come to an end by a move of the Holy Spirit.

This period of two thousand years was kept secret to the prophets. Yet the end of it was foretold in Joel, when he said that God would pour out His Spirit upon His servants, both men and women (Joel 2:28,29). That happened at the beginning of this century when the latter rain of the Holy Spirit came down to earth in the Pentecostal outpouring. Soon that work of the Holy Spirit will cease, and the harvest time will begin, though we don't know at what hour.

Around the time when this gospel age and the period of the Spirit's outpouring have come near to an end, Israel has risen again, regaining her nationhood. The fig tree is a symbol of Israel, and Jesus said: "Now learn the parable from the fig tree: when its branch has already become tender, and puts forth its leaves, you know that summer is near; even so you too, when you see all these things, recognize that He is near, right at the door" (Matt. 24:32,33).

The fig tree, Israel, wandered among the nations for a long time but has finally become a nation once more and put forth leaves. Before long the ten countries of Europe will be united and one ruler will come out of them. He will conclude the seven-year treaty with Israel. With the conclusion of the treaty, both the church age and the time of the Gentiles will end. Then will start the time when God gives the final exhortation to the Jewish nation.

Listen to the news that comes today from Europe, and you will realize how accurately and swiftly these scriptures are being fulfilled. Not much time is left to preach the gospel. We don't know exactly how many years are left, but we can be sure that we are now standing at the threshold of the end times.

9

Daniel's Prophecy of Seventy Weeks

Jeremiah's Prophecy (9:1-2)

In the first year of Darius the son of Ahasuerus, of Median descent, who was made king over the kingdom of the Chaldeans—in the first year of his reign I, Daniel, observed in the books the number of the years which was revealed as the word of the Lord to Jeremiah the prophet for the completion of the desolations of Jerusalem, namely, seventy years.

We should note that, even though Daniel had such deep revelation from God, he did not neglect the study of the Scriptures. In contrast, when some people pray and receive a little bit of revelation from God in answer to their prayers, they talk big about this and that, based solely on the revelation, laying aside the Bible.

The books or scrolls Daniel saw here refer to Jeremiah. While he read the prophet prayerfully in order to find out what would happen to Israel in the future, he came across a passage with a wonderful promise in it:

> 'Moreover, I will take from them the voice of joy and the voice of gladness, the voice of the bridegroom and the voice of the bride, the sound of the millstones and the light of the lamp. And this whole land shall be a desolation and a horror, and these nations shall serve the king of Babylon seventy years. Then it will be when seventy years are completed I will punish the king of Babylon and that nation,' declares the Lord, 'for their iniquity, and the land of the Chaldeans; and I will make it an everlasting desolation' (Jer. 25:10-12).

This prophecy said that Israel would be taken captive to serve the Babylonian kings for seventy years. It also predicted that after that period, when God's appointed time was fulfilled, God would punish Babylon and grant freedom to Israel. So Daniel was deeply moved by this passage.

As we noted before, the primary reason the Israelites were carried away as captives and had to suffer for seventy years was that they had repeatedly broken the Sabbath. So God repaid them for their deed. The Sabbath law had three strict stipulations.

First, the people were to work for six days, but on the seventh day they had to cease from work. Second, after having kept a fellow Israelite as a slave for six years, they had to set him or her free in the seventh year. And third, when they plowed a field, they might plow it for six years, but in the seventh year they had to let it lie fallow. God promised a harvest that would provide Israel extra provisions to support them during this fallow year if they would obey this command.

But the Israelites habitually broke all the Sabbath laws. So God allowed the nation to be taken captive and exiled so that the land, which had been denied its Sabbath up to that time, could rest for seventy years.

We must recognize that the commandment to work for six days and rest on the seventh was not given to afflict us but to bring us benefit. This is the law of the God who created the universe and who knows what is best for us. So today we should also live according to this divine law. Otherwise, compulsory rest will come to us as it came to Israel when the nation was sent into captivity for seventy years.

Daniel felt his heart burning when he read the verse from the prophet which promised that his people would return home from captivity after seventy years, once the land had rested and the Jews had repented of their ways. The day when he could go home was drawing near. All that remained was for the people to repent, so Daniel began to intercede for his people.

The Secret of Acceptable Prayer (9:3,4)

So I gave my attention to the Lord God to seek Him by prayer and supplications, with fasting, sackcloth, and ashes. And I prayed to the Lord my God and confessed and said, "Alas, O Lord, the great and awesome God, who keeps His covenant and lovingkindness for those who love Him and keep His commandments...."

Daniel's prayer was extraordinary. Whenever I read it I can feel his heart, torn to pieces and bleeding for his nation. It was a prayer accepted by God.

We should learn from Daniel's example the secret of prayer which is acceptable to God. Whatever divine promise we may have, unless we pray, it cannot come true. Prayer is an essential condition for the fulfillment of the divine promise.

Through the prophet Jeremiah, God had no doubt promised Israel that after seventy years He would destroy the king of

Babylon and send the Israelites home. This promise, however, rested on the premise that God's people had first to understand the divine promise and then to pray. The promise was not an unconditional one that would be automatically fulfilled.

Even though the Bible has as many as 32,500 promises, they can be fulfilled only when we know about them and pray for their fulfillment, as Daniel did. If we assume an indifferent attitude, saying, "May this be done as You will," not a single promise will be fulfilled in our lifetime. The creative work of God will not take place until the promise of God, which comes down from heaven, and the prayer of God's people, which goes up from earth, meet and join together.

Daniel's Extra Efforts

After Daniel knew the promise of God recorded in Jeremiah, he resolved to plead with God fervently. He did not want to do a halfhearted job.

We must pray the same way today. Without firm resolve in our prayer, we cannot receive an answer. If we pray half-heartedly, just saying, "Amen, we believe," our prayer will not rise up to heaven before God.

To ensure that God would answer his prayer without fail, Daniel made some extra efforts. The first one was fasting. The truly powerful prayer is one joined with fasting. When we pray earnestly, even to the extent of restraining our strong human instinct for eating, our prayer will not fail to rise to God. But if we pray while still satisfying our desire for food and sleep, our prayer cannot go beyond the level of an ordinary petition.

The second extra effort was sackcloth. By putting away comfortable clothing and putting on coarse cloth, Daniel showed that he was thoroughly repenting. In fact, he went one step further to humble himself: He prayed with ashes on his head.

The kind of firm resolve Daniel had is an essential part of an acceptable prayer to God. Especially when we pray about a critical problem that faces us, we cannot break the strength of the devil unless we are prepared to plead with God in prayer and in petition, in fasting, sackcloth and ashes.

Daniel's Confession of Sins (9:5,6)

"...we have sinned, committed iniquity, acted wickedly, and rebelled, even turning aside from Thy commandments and ordinances. Moreover, we have not listened to Thy servants the prophets, who spoke in Thy name to our kings, our princes, our fathers, and all the people of the land."

In three aspects, Daniel's prayer sets an example for us. The first aspect is the confession of sins.

No human being lives without sin. The Bible says, "There is none righteous, not even one....For all have sinned and fall short of the glory of God" (Rom. 3:10,23).

It is not sinners who are sent to hell by God; rather it is those sinners who do not repent. So the most dreadful thing is not sin, but the impenitent heart.

For that reason, when we come to God we must first pray penitently, confessing our sins. When God sees us turning to Him, confessing our sins, He does not forsake us. Instead He has compassion on the contrite heart that seeks His forgiveness.

Listen to Daniel's prayer of repentance. Perhaps no one was more faithful to God than Daniel, who maintained the integrity of his faith. But he chose to bear upon his shoulders in confession not only his own sin, but the sins of all the Jews.

We should learn to imitate Daniel's attitude. Like him, we should confess not only our own sins, but the sins of our country

121

and our people as well.

Daniel said in his prayer, "We have sinned, committed iniquity, acted wickedly, and rebelled, even turning aside from Thy commandments and ordinances" (v. 5). What is our sin? It is violation of the law of God. If we know the law of God and yet break it, we commit a sin.

Daniel also confessed the sin of indifference which the people committed against the word of the Lord. He said that the Jews had not only broken God's laws; they had also failed to listen to God's servants, the prophets. Daniel repents especially on behalf of past leaders of Israel, lamenting bitterly as if it were his own sin.

In order to offer acceptable prayer to God, we too must examine ourselves to determine whether we are breaking the law of God. Then, if we find that we are, we must confess it. In addition, we should confess not only our own sin but also the sins of our family members when we bring them to God in prayer.

Confession is essential to our spiritual life. When some people today try to receive the Holy Spirit, they fall victim instead to an evil spirit because they do not make thorough confession of sins before they pray to receive the Spirit. Because sin still remains in the hearts of these people, the Holy Spirit cannot enter. To make matters worse, because their hearts are wide open, an evil spirit may enter, seeking after sin, to oppress their hearts.

For that reason, when we come to Jesus Christ to receive special grace after we are forgiven of our sins through faith in Him, we must first confess all the sins we can remember and wash them away with the precious blood of Jesus. If we put on purity when we pray to God, the devil cannot enter our hearts.

The devil is just like a fly. He hates clean places. Just as we remove a dirty garbage can to keep flies from gathering around it in our homes, we should treat sins as if they were garbage cans, removing them from our hearts. If we fail to do this, we have no reason to complain of being tempted by the devil.

The Prayer of a Broken Heart (9:7-15)

"Righteousness belongs to Thee, O Lord, but to us open shame, as it is this day—to the men of Judah, the inhabitants of Jerusalem, and all Israel, those who are nearby and those who are far away in all the countries to which Thou hast driven them, because of their unfaithful deeds which they have committed against Thee. Open shame belongs to us, O Lord, to our kings, our princes, and our fathers, because we have sinned against Thee. To the Lord our God belong compassion and forgiveness, for we have rebelled against Him; nor have we obeyed the voice of the Lord our God, to walk in His teachings which He set before us through His servants the prophets. Indeed all Israel has transgressed Thy law and turned aside, not obeying Thy voice; so the curse has been poured out on us, along with the oath which is written in the law of Moses the servant of God, for we have sinned against Him. Thus He has confirmed His words which He had spoken against us and against our rulers who ruled us, to bring on us great calamity; for under the whole heaven there has not been done anything like what was done to Jerusalem. As it is written in the law of Moses, all this calamity has come on us; yet we have not sought the favor of the Lord our God by turning from our iniquity and giving attention to Thy truth. Therefore, the Lord has kept the calamity

in store and brought it on us; for the Lord our God is righteous with respect to all His deeds which He has done, but we have not obeyed His voice. And now, O Lord our God, who hast brought Thy people out of the land of Egypt with a mighty hand and hast made a name for Thyself, as it is this day—we have sinned, we have been wicked.''

A second aspect of Daniel's prayer is that it is the prayer of a broken heart. He was so ashamed of the sins of his people that he could only cry out that Israel deserved the shame and disgrace to which it was subjected. He pointed out Israel's stubbornness, admitting that even though Jerusalem itself had become a ruin by the unprecedented judgment of God, Israel deserved the judgment: The nation had neither repented nor sought God's grace even down to the last moment when it was carried away to a heathen country.

Do you know what true repentance is? It requires that we avoid making an excuse for our sin or complaining about the present ill we may be suffering because of our sin. Those who are genuinely penitent say: "Lord, I deserve this trouble I have. Righteousness belongs to You, but to me the punishment. Yet, in comparison with the sin I have committed, even this is rather a light punishment. Thank You.'' A prayer like this is a prayer coming from a broken heart.

Prayer for Forgiveness and Restoration (9:16-19)

"O Lord, in accordance with all Thy righteous acts, let now Thine anger and Thy wrath turn away from Thy city Jerusalem, Thy holy mountain; for because of our sins and the iniquities of our fathers, Jerusalem and Thy people have become a reproach to all those around us.

So now, our God, listen to the prayer of Thy servant and to his supplications, and for Thy sake, O Lord, let Thy face shine on Thy desolate sanctuary. O my God, incline Thine ear and hear! Open Thine eyes and see our desolations and the city which is called by Thy name; for we are not presenting our supplications before Thee on account of any merits of our own, but on account of Thy great compassion. O Lord, hear! O Lord, forgive! O Lord, listen and take action! For Thine own sake, O my God, do not delay, because Thy city and Thy people are called by Thy name."

Third, Daniel prayed entreating God's forgiveness and restoration. He appealed to the righteous acts God had performed for the Jews up to that time. So even though the nation was suffering its deserved shame, he pleaded with God to remember the holy city Jerusalem and to have mercy on it. And he asked God to restore the ruined sanctuary for His own sake.

In all these ways, then, we should pray as Daniel did, keeping in mind the aspects of his prayer we have discussed. And when we pray a prayer of confession, we should not get our prayer out of focus by being distracted. We must make our prayer succinct, reflecting these three elements illustrated by Daniel's prayer.

In addition, we should make a thorough confession of sins for our family and our country. The Bible clearly tells us:

Behold, the Lord's hand is not so short
That it cannot save;
Neither is his ear so dull
That it cannot hear.
But your iniquities have made a separation between you
and your God, and your sins have hidden His face from

you, so that He does not hear (Is. 59:1-2).

Finally, we should beg God to give us an opportunity to live exerting our utmost effort for the Lord's name and His glory. "Only for the Lord"—this should be the central theme of our final supplication.

I pray in Jesus' name that you too may learn to pray as Daniel did.

Gabriel's Answer to Daniel's Prayer (9:20-23)

Now while I was speaking and praying, and confessing my sin and the sin of my people Israel, and presenting my supplication before the Lord my God in behalf of the holy mountain of my God, while I was still speaking in prayer, then the man Gabriel, whom I had seen in the vision previously, came to me in my extreme weariness about the time of the evening offering. And he gave me instruction and talked with me, and said, "O Daniel, I have now come forth to give you insight with understanding. At the beginning of your supplications the command was issued, and I have come to tell you, for you are highly esteemed; so give heed to the message and gain understanding of the vision."

Daniel's prayer was so well prepared and firmly based on the three elements we have discussed that the divine answer could not but come down from the throne of God. The archangel Gabriel was sent to bring that answer to Daniel.

The recorded prayer of Daniel is brief because it is only the gist of what he prayed. Actually, Daniel prayed all day long, from morning until the evening sacrifice. Then about the time of the evening sacrifice Gabriel appeared.

According to the Bible, Jacob had a dream in which he saw

a stairway resting on the earth with its top reaching to heaven and angels of God ascending and descending on it (Gen. 28:12). These angels of God, who travel back and forth between heaven and earth, number more than ten thousand times ten thousand, and they are His ministering spirits sent out to render service to God's people (Heb. 1:14). So when we pray to God, God answers our prayer by sending these hosts of heaven.

Whenever we pray an appropriate prayer to God, God's command is immediately given. But it takes time for angels to bring it to us. God is omniscient, omnipotent and omnipresent, but angels are not. So don't get discouraged even when you fail to receive a quick answer to your prayer.

Daniel's Seventy Years (9:24-27)

"Seventy weeks have been decreed for your people and your holy city, to finish the transgression, to make an end of sin, to make atonement for iniquity, to bring in everlasting righteousness, to seal up vision and prophecy, and to anoint the most holy place" (v. 24).

When Gabriel came to Daniel with God's answer to his prayer, he spoke about the seventy weeks in Jeremiah's prophecy. This short passage illuminates a great deal of biblical history and provides a key to the understanding of the entire Bible.

If we had to read the passage alone with no one to explain it to us, we would find it the most difficult puzzle in the world. But when we read these words in the light of what we have studied so far in the previous chapters of Daniel and with what we are told in the book of Revelation, their meaning is fully revealed.

As we can see from Gabriel's opening words of interpretation (v. 24), this prophecy centers upon the Jewish nation. I believe this is because the history of God's people as recorded in the Bible always serves as a clock for the history of the entire world. That is, just as we look at a clock to know the time, so we must look at the history of the Jews to understand the timing of world history, for God reveals the history of the world through the Jewish nation.

Because a week is composed of seven days, the term "seventy weeks" here means seventy times seven days, or 490 days. What is the significance of this 490 days?

According to the book of Numbers, when the spies returned from the land of Canaan after exploring it for forty days, they gave a bad report about the land so that the Israelites who heard them grumbled against God. For this reason, God was enraged and sent Israel back into the wilderness, saying, "According to the number of days which you spied out the land, forty days, for every day you shall bear your guilt a year, even forty years, and you shall know My opposition" (Num. 14:34).

Using the same formula for calculating the length of Israel's judgment in Jeremiah's time, seventy weeks or 490 days would refer to 490 years. The following verses indicate that there will be sixty-nine weeks from the decree to rebuild and restore Jerusalem until the time of the Messiah. The last week, the seventieth week, refers to the great tribulation that is yet to occur. In all, seventy weeks or 490 years are determined for the period from the return of the Jews from captivity to the millennial kingdom started by the return of Jesus Christ to this world. In all these ways, 490 is a providential and historical number for the Jews.

What Will Happen After 490 Years?

The Bible says that the transgression of the entire nation of the Jews would be finished after seventy weeks, or 490 years.

This time was decreed to finish all the transgressions of Israel committed against God, to put an end to the sin which originated with Adam and Eve and to atone for wickedness forever.

These things took place when sins were destroyed once and for all by the precious blood of Jesus Christ which He shed on the cross, and everlasting righteousness was brought in. At that time all the visions and prophecies were sealed. Now, after all these things have taken place, Jesus Christ is to be anointed and is to come again to take over the earth. Then at last the world will be completely changed into the kingdom of God.

Therefore, those who criticize the Bible today must be silent before this prophecy of Daniel. If the Bible were a book not recorded by divine revelation, but fabricated by human beings, then how could Daniel, writing twenty-six hundred years ago, pinpoint events that would happen in our own age and are still to happen in the future? Certainly Daniel did not prophesy past things, but rather future things.

The Commandment to Restore and to Build Jerusalem

"So you are to know and discern that from the issuing of a decree to restore and rebuild Jerusalem until Messiah the Prince there will be seven weeks and sixty-two weeks; it will be built again, with plaza and moat, even in times of distress" *(v. 25).*

The Messiah of this passage refers to Christ. These words tell about the first coming of Jesus.

Gabriel told Daniel that the anointed king would be born in Israel after seven weeks and sixty-two weeks, or sixty-nine weeks. During the first seven weeks Jerusalem would be restored and rebuilt, and the king would be born sixty-two weeks after that time. So our concern must be to determine when the commandment was given to restore and rebuild Jerusalem.

In Ezra 1:1 we read that the decree to restore and rebuild Jerusalem was issued in the first year of King Cyrus of Persia. The words of the decree are recorded there:

> *Now in the first year of Cyrus king of Persia, in order to fulfill the word of the Lord by the mouth of Jeremiah, the Lord stirred up the spirit of Cyrus king of Persia, so that he sent a proclamation throughout all his kingdom, and also put it in writing, saying, "Thus says Cyrus king of Persia, 'The Lord, the God of heaven, has given me all the kingdoms of the earth, and He has appointed me to build Him a house in Jerusalem, which is in Judah. Whoever there is among you of all His people, may his God be with him! Let him go up to Jerusalem which is in Judah, and rebuild the house of the Lord, the God of Israel; He is the God who is in Jerusalem. And every survivor, at whatever place he may live, let the men of that place support him with silver and gold, with goods and cattle, together with a freewill offering for the house of God which is in Jerusalem (Ezra 1:1-4).*

Thus Cyrus's decree to allow the Jews to return to their native land was the divine answer to Daniel's prayer. As prophesied by Jeremiah, exactly seventy years after the exile, God had Cyrus of Persia issue the decree to send the Jews to their native land, allowing them to restore and rebuild the sanctuary—but not the city of Jerusalem.

Yet the prophecy which came to Daniel tells us that the date of the Messiah's appearance must be calculated from the date of the issuance of the decree to restore and rebuild Jerusalem. This was given in the month of Nisan in the twentieth year of

King Artaxerxes. Converted to dates on our modern calendar, this corresponds to March 14, 445 B.C. We can know this from Nehemiah chapters 1 and 2.

Daniel's prophecy says that there will be seven weeks and sixty-two weeks from the issuance of the decree to restore and to rebuild Jerusalem until the coming of the Anointed One, the ruler. The Hebrew word for week can also be translated "seven." Sixty-nine "weeks" could also be understood to mean sixty-nine sevens. Calculate this for yourself:

(7 years x 7) + (62 years x 7) = 483 years.

The prophecy says that Jerusalem would be rebuilt "with plaza and moat" in seven sevens. Later those words came to pass: It did actually take seven sevens, or forty-nine years, for Jerusalem to be restored.

In addition, the prophecy says that the Anointed One, the Messiah, will come when sixty-two weeks had passed. This was also fulfilled in history. Sixty-two weeks represents 434 years; and 434 years after Jerusalem was restored and rebuilt, Jesus entered Jerusalem riding on a donkey, where a large crowd gathered to welcome Him as a king. This is the day we call Palm Sunday.

Daniel's prophecy even shows the accurate date of Jesus' entry into Jerusalem. On the Jewish calendar, one year was 360 days instead of 365 days (as in our present calendar). Leap year came around every four years as it does now. If we add seven weeks and sixty-two weeks—that is, 483 years—to March 14, 445 B.C. (the month of Nisan, the twentieth year of King Artaxerxes), taking into account the necessary adjustments for the differences in calendars, we get April 6, 32 A.D. This is the approximate time, if not the very day, when Jesus entered Jerusalem as a king. Praise the Lord! If Daniel's prophecies had not been a true revelation from God, they could not have been so precisely accurate.

Then after the sixty-two weeks the Messiah will be cut off and have nothing (v. 26a).

The prophecy further says that after the sixty-two weeks, the Anointed One would be cut off. Thus Daniel even predicted our Lord's crucifixion.

But why would the Messiah, that is, Christ the Son of God, be cut off as soon as He entered Jerusalem as the king? This king did not die because of His own sin. He voluntarily bore our wickedness, our vileness, our despair and our curse. He died on the cross by His own free will to prepare an eternal place for us. How amazing is the Lord's grace!

The People of the Prince That Shall Come

And the people of the prince who is to come will destroy the city and the sanctuary. And its end will come with a flood; even to the end there will be war; desolations are determined (v. 26b).

According to Daniel's vision, after the Messiah was cut off, Jerusalem and the sanctuary would be destroyed. This actually happened in A.D. 70. After the crucifixion of Jesus, the Jews rebelled against Rome to obtain freedom, but the revolt was quickly quelled by a Roman army dispatched under the leadership of Titus. The prophecy goes on to say that the end will come like a flood, war will continue until the end, and desolations have been decreed. While suppressing the revolt, the Roman army destroyed Jerusalem so completely that no stone was left on another. It is said that half a million Jewish youths were killed in this revolt against the Romans, and blood ran like a river in Jerusalem.

As we said before, because the church age—that is, the time from the first coming of Christ to His second coming—has nothing to do with the history of the Jews, God removed it from the prophecy of the Jews.

Of these seventy weeks prophesied by Daniel, the first sixty-nine weeks are already fulfilled: Jerusalem was restored and rebuilt during the seven weeks; sixty-two weeks after that the Anointed One, Jesus Christ, appeared and was cut off; and "the people of the prince," namely Titus, the Roman general, destroyed Jerusalem. During the following two thousand years, humanity has lived in a world which has become desolate by a succession of wars like the coming of a flood.

The Last Week

"And he will make a firm covenant with the many for one week, but in the middle of the week he will put a stop to sacrifice and grain offering; and on the wing of abominations will come one who makes desolate, even until a complete destruction, one that is decreed, is poured out on the one who makes desolate" (v. 27).

Suddenly there appears in verse 27 a single week. This one week refers to seven years.

Who then is the one who will "make a firm covenant with the many"? Considered in context, "he" refers to "the prince" in verse 26—that is, the Roman leader. Rome no longer exists now. So how can the Roman leader come and confirm the covenant with the Jews for seven years? Actually, we have already examined this mystery.

Remember the age of the toes of the golden image which King Nebuchadnezzar saw and the age of the ten horns of the fourth beast which Daniel saw? They both signify the ten nations in a unified Europe that will rise again in the former territory of Rome. As we have seen, today is the last age, and the unification of ten nations is rapidly taking place in the former territory of Rome.

When a unified Europe is thus achieved, the antichrist referred to in verse 27 will arise from it. He will confirm a covenant with many, which refers to the Jewish nation. But it was necessary that Israel first regain its status as a nation to bring forth the fulfillment of this seven-year treaty.

As recently as half a century ago, the Jews were still a wandering people in exile. At that time the last week of Daniel's seventy weeks must have seemed like a dream. But now all that has changed: Israel is once again a nation after being reborn in 1948, and it is waiting for confirmation of the treaty of seven years.

"In the midst of the week" (v. 27) refers to the same period that John calls "a time and times and half a time" in Revelation (12:14)—that is, the first three and half years. When these three and a half years pass, the antichrist will put an end to sacrifices and offerings in the temple at Jerusalem. And in a wing of the temple he will set up an abomination that will cause desolation.

As we have seen before, he will set up his own statue in the temple to deify himself. Then he will force the Jews to bow down to the idol or else be put to death. But the Jews who have kept the law of Moses will defy the command, and a brutal massacre will follow.

Referring to this time, Jesus said there would be a great distress, unequalled from the beginning of the world. But only through such a tragic and painful tribulation will the Jews be finally broken so that they surrender themselves to Jesus Christ as their Savior.

Finally, God's wrath will be poured out, and when the second half of the tribulation ends, Jesus Christ will come down to the earth to judge it and begin the millennial reign.

We now live at the end of the last age. Watch and pray. You do not know exactly when the Bridegroom will come (see Matt. 25:1-13). But since the night is far spent, the coming of the Bridegroom must be imminent. You must be ready to partake of the wedding supper of the Lamb.

When the Lord himself comes down from heaven with a loud command, with the voice of the archangel and the trumpet call of God, you will be changed and be caught up together in the clouds with the dead in Christ who have risen first to meet the Lord in the air (1 Thess. 4:16,17). So make sure there is oil in your lamp.

10

The War in the Spiritual World

Daniel's Final Vision (10:1-9)

In the third year of Cyrus king of Persia a message was revealed to Daniel, who was named Belteshazzar; and the message was true and one of great conflict, but he understood the message and had an understanding of the vision. In those days I, Daniel, had been mourning for three entire weeks. I did not eat any tasty food, nor did meat or wine enter my mouth, nor did I use any ointment at all, until the entire three weeks were completed. And on the twenty-fourth day of the first month, while I was by the bank of the great river, that is, the Tigris... (vv. 1-4).

For three weeks Daniel mourned and prayed while observing a partial fast. The revelation he then received, recorded in chapter 11, was about war in the spiritual world. On the other hand, the revelation in chapter 12 concerned war in the human world.

By this time Daniel was eighty-six years old. If he still had

137

any lingering hopes, they were probably for the restoration and rebuilding of Jerusalem and the temple, and the return of the Jews to their native land. In fact, three years before this time Ezra and Nehemiah had led the Jews back to their homeland to restore the nation. But Daniel continuously received news that the work of rebuilding the temple was being delayed by the interference and false accusations of countries neighboring Judah. So when Daniel heard this news, he became so distressed that he made up his mind to pray for the salvation of his native land.

Consequently, Daniel and several others went to the Hiddekel River, which is now called the Tigris River, to pray. He ate no choice food until the three weeks were over. Since he was almost ninety years old, he was too feeble for a total fast. In the same way, if anyone finds today that total fasting is too hard, that person should try a partial fast—that is, limited eating.

Daniel abstained not only from choice food, but also from meat and wine. He ate only plain food, and just enough to keep himself alive. In addition, he refrained from anointing himself and dressing up.

Here we need to look at the scene behind the stage of the physical world—that is, the spiritual world. More often than not we lose heart in prayer, concluding that the answer will not come. But our Lord wants us to recognize what is happening in the spiritual world so we can have hope to wait just a little longer.

Our prayer is our struggle. When we fight on the earth, the angel who has the answer of God for us also fights in the air. Between humanity and the throne of God, the devil, who is the prince of the air, is encamped. His demons are desperately endeavoring to block our prayers from reaching heaven.

Nevertheless, if we keep praying on the earth, the angel will catch the cord of our prayer and come to us, breaking through the stronghold of the devil. This is what happened to Daniel. A full twenty-one days had passed before he received an answer to his prayer.

The Angel Who Came

...I lifted my eyes and looked, and behold, there was a certain man dressed in linen, whose waist was girded with a belt of pure gold of Uphaz. His body also was like beryl, his face had the appearance of lightning, his eyes were like flaming torches, his arms and feet like the gleam of polished bronze, and the sound of his words like the sound of a tumult. Now I, Daniel, alone saw the vision, while the men who were with me did not see the vision; nevertheless, a great dread fell on them, and they ran away to hide themselves. So I was left alone and saw this great vision; yet no strength was left in me, for my natural color turned to a deathly pallor, and I retained no strength. But I heard the sound of his words; and as soon as I heard the sound of his words, I fell into a deep sleep on my face, with my face to the ground (vv. 5-9).

The angel who came to Daniel with an answer to his prayer must have had a very high position. His appearance, as Daniel described it, was dazzling, even overwhelming. But even though the description sounds somewhat like John's description of Jesus in Revelation, it was not Jesus who appeared to Daniel. If it had been Jesus, He could have come quickly, penetrating the encampment of the devil. But since it was an angel, he was detained by the devil for twenty-one days before he finally came.

Daniel saw the angel because his spiritual eyes were open.

139

But those who prayed with him did not see the angel, although they were so terrified that they fled and hid themselves. Sometimes we find ourselves in the same situation as those men. Though nothing is to be seen in the room where we are, it seems as if we can actually feel the presence of the Lord. At other times while we are praying, we feel as though an angel is at our side.

The War in the Spiritual World (10:10-21)

Then behold, a hand touched me and set me trembling on my hands and knees. And he said to me, "O Daniel, man of high esteem, understand the words that I am about to tell you and stand upright, for I have now been sent to you." And when he had spoken this word to me, I stood up trembling (vv. 10,11).

The angel refreshed Daniel and set him on his feet so that he could hear clearly the angel's detailed explanation about the war in the spiritual world. This war is described in only one other place in the Bible:

For our struggle is not against flesh and blood, but against the rulers, against the powers, against the world forces of this darkness, against the spiritual forces of wickedness in the heavenly places (Eph. 6:12).

Our faith can be successful only when we fully grasp this secret of the spiritual world.

Then he said to me, "Do not be afraid, Daniel, for from the first day that you set your heart on understanding this and on humbling yourself before your God, your words were heard, and I have come in response to your words. But the prince of the kingdom of Persia was withstanding me for twenty-one days; then behold, Michael, one of the chief princes, came to help me, for I had been left there with the kings of Persia. Now I have come to give you an understanding of what will happen to your people in the latter days, for the vision pertains to the days yet future." And when he had spoken to me according to these words, I turned my face toward the ground and became speechless. And behold, one who resembled a human being was touching my lips; then I opened my mouth and spoke, and said to him who was standing before me, "O my lord, as a result of the vision anguish has come upon me, and I have retained no strength. For how can such a servant of my lord talk with such as my lord? As for me, there remains just now no strength in me, nor has any breath been left in me."

Then this one with human appearance touched me again and strengthened me. And he said, "O man of high esteem, do not be afraid. Peace be with you; take courage and be courageous!" Now as soon as he spoke to me, I received strength and said, "May my lord speak, for you have strengthened me" (vv. 12-19).

We should note that on the very first day Daniel set his mind to gain understanding and to humble himself before God, Daniel's words were heard and the angel came in response to them. When we repent of our sins, admitting that the judgment God has passed upon us is a just one, and humbly beg God for His mercy, God's answer will come swiftly in response to our prayer.

Nevertheless, it took twenty-one days for the angel to come to Daniel. We read here that the prince of the Persian kingdom resisted the angel twenty-one days so that the angel was detained. The king of Persia was a human being who lived on the earth. How then was it possible for the angel of heaven to be detained for twenty-one days by a human being?

Here lies a deep secret of the spiritual world. We must realize that behind this earthly king of Persia was a demonic force also called the king of Persia. The demons were encamped in the air over that throne, and they took possession of the king of Persia and his people, exercising strong influence over them.

On the first day Daniel started his prayer, which continued for the following three weeks accompanied by a partial fast, the cord of his prayer went up to heaven, and God sent an angel in response to his prayer. But the devil obstructed the passage of the angel with all his might, for he was afraid that he might lose his domain by the advancement of the kingdom of God.

From this we know that behind the human kingdoms of the earth there is always a struggle between the demons and the angels of God. For that reason we Christians must view rulers such as Kim Il-sung, chieftain of the present North Korean puppet regime, in the light of this spiritual reality. Kim is notorious for his cruelty and wickedness, even in the communist bloc, and we should not be surprised that behind him is the prince of his kingdom, encamped in the air. The fact is that the devil is behind Kim Il-sung, manipulating him.

Consequently, the way to bring down Kim Il-sung's communist regime is to compel the angel of God to bring God's answer to us through our fasting and prayer—before we resort to military arms. The object of our spiritual struggle is the devil who manipulates Kim Il-sung. If our prayer is brought up to God, and the angel of God comes down to take prisoner the prince of the communist nations in response to our prayer, communism will be brought low like a castle of sand.

Such prayer warfare is being waged even now. The Kim Il-sung regime has kept a vigilant eye on the Republic of Korea to invade it, but it has not been able to succeed these thirty-eight years since the Korean War—for it has always been ensnared by its own trap. The prayers which the faithful Christians pray day and night in the mountain and in the field, in the closet and in the church, have bound our true enemy, the devil, who is behind Kim Il-sung. This is a sign that because of our prayer the devil who manipulates Kim Il-sung will be defeated by the angel of heaven. Whatever strategy Kim Il-sung may use, he will be kept at bay in the future as long as our prayers continue, for the prince of Kim Il-sung has already been defeated by the angel of God.

Though the angel was resisted for twenty-one days by the prince of Persia, the unceasing prayers of Daniel on the earth allowed Michael—who was in charge of God's army—to come. Backed up by his help, the angel was able to defeat the prince of Persia and come down to Daniel after three weeks.

With this scene in mind we should remember that throughout all the ages those who pray for their country and their people are the true patriots, men and women of prayer who have fervently dedicated themselves to a vigil of fasting and prayer. We should pray day and night for the leaders of our country. And in order to deliver our twenty million compatriots suffering in North Korea, we Christians in South Korea should pray first that God's angels in heaven may defeat the demons who are behind North Korea, winning the victory in the war of the spiritual sphere.

In a similar way, when we are praying for the repentance of family members, we should also take the victory in the war of the spiritual world. Exhortation and persuasion with worldly wisdom cannot bear any fruit. For example, a spirit of rebellion and defiance will cause children to be even more resistant to authority when parents discipline them.

At such times, parents should pray that the demons who are behind their children be cast out. A person is completely changed when the demons are cast out and the Spirit of God comes in. The Bible says that, when Philip preached the gospel to a city in Samaria, evil spirits came out of many with shrieks, and many paralytics and cripples were healed (Acts 8:5-8). Today evil spirits must first be cast out to heal those who are paralyzed and crippled spiritually and make them children of God.

In order to make a nation stand upright, the evil prince which is behind the nation must be driven away through prayer. The demon which seeks to steal and kill an individual or a family must also be bound through prayer. After healing a boy possessed with a demon, Jesus said, "But this kind does not go out except by prayer and fasting" (Matt. 17:21, marginal note).

Above all things, we Christians must first start with prayer to break the stronghold of demons. Then the Spirit of God will come to indwell us, and the angels of the Lord will attend us. If we achieve victory in the spiritual war so that the inner person of the one we are praying for is changed, that person will be a good Christian and will love God. A child will obey his or her parents; a spouse will have a love for family members and neighbors.

The apostle Paul taught us how to win a sure victory without fail in such a battle: "With all prayer and petition pray at all times in the Spirit, and with this in view, be on the alert with all perseverance and petition for all the saints" (Eph. 6:18). Whoever wins in this battle of prayer for the spiritual world also wins in the physical world. Whoever loses in the battle of prayer also becomes a loser in the physical world.

The War Continues Today

Then he said, "Do you understand why I came to you?

But I shall now return to fight against the prince of Persia; so I am going forth, and behold, the prince of Greece is about to come. However, I will tell you what is inscribed in the writing of truth. Yet there is no one who stands firmly with me against these forces except Michael your prince" (vv. 20,21).

The angel of God fought with the prince of Persia, but his fight did not end there. He fought with the prince of Greece as well, and his fight will continue with the kingdom of Satan and with his power to the end of the world. So we should pray unceasingly to help angels win in the spiritual war.

The individual who prays will no more fall than the family or the nation who prays. But the nation which fights only in the physical world is bound to fall.

It is no accident that Korea has 10,000,000 Christians. I believe God wants to use the Korean church to send out missionaries to every nation and people in the world to preach the gospel that they may be saved through repentance. So the Korean church must cease denominational contention, which is utterly destructive, and concentrate its efforts instead to pray that the nation may more abundantly receive grace and be filled with the Spirit, that the fire of revival may grow. And we should also pray that the Korean church may become united.

Christians in every land would do well to pray the same way. We are all generals engaged in spiritual war, and Michael, the captain of God's host, stands by our side.

11

The Kings of the South and the North

Persia and Greece (11:1-4)

"And in the first year of Darius the Mede, I arose to be an encouragement and a protection for him. And now I will tell you the truth. Behold, three more kings are going to arise in Persia. Then a fourth will gain far more riches than all of them; as soon as he becomes strong through his riches, he will arouse the whole empire against the realm of Greece" (vv. 1,2).

Chapter 11 begins with an interesting statement by the angel. He said that he had stood with Darius the Mede to confirm and strengthen him in his first year as king. Now let's think for a minute about the meaning of this passage.

When the Medo-Persians conquered Babylon and set up their kingdom, the demons took possession of this kingdom and manipulated it to try to destroy all the captive Jews within its borders. As their first measure the demons stirred up all the administrators and satraps of the kingdom to bring charges

147

against Daniel to King Darius. They probably intended to begin an extensive extermination against the Jews as soon as Daniel was killed in the den of lions. But thanks to Daniel's prayer, the angels of God defeated the demons who were in possession of the kingdom so that an angel could get into the lions' den and shut their mouths.

Consequently, King Darius was so impressed by this incident that he afterward began to adopt a pro-Jewish policy. He ordered that the administrators who had accused Daniel be thrown into the lions' den along with all their households. And he issued a decree to all the people in the kingdom that they should worship Daniel's God.

Thus the Jews could live well, even in the land where they had been carried as captives, because an angel took his stand to support King Darius and strengthen him.

The Kings Who Will Appear in Persia

Now let's pay attention to the words of the prophecy itself. The prophecy first tells about the kings who would appear in Persia. It was in fact fulfilled in later history.

The first king who appeared was Cambyses (529-522 B.C.); the second king was Pseudo-Smerdis (522-521 B.C.); and the third was Darius I Hystaspes (521-486 B.C.). The fourth king was Xerxes I, who reigned from 486-465 B.C. During his reign Persia reached its highest glory. Xerxes was also called Ahasuerus and was the same king who appeared in the book of Esther.

At the time of the fourth king, the Medo-Persian kingdom—which had become extremely rich—set up a strategy to invade Greece. After a four-year preparation, the empire mobilized an army of one million. The army set out on its campaign against Greece in 480 B.C. but was defeated in humiliation by Greece.

As a result, Persia began to decline after Xerxes I and finally fell to the Greeks.

A Mighty King Who Is to Come

"And a mighty king will arise, and he will rule with great authority and do as he pleases. But as soon as he has arisen, his kingdom will be broken up and parceled out toward the four points of the compass, though not to his own descendants, nor according to his authority which he wielded; for his sovereignty will be uprooted and given to others besides them" (vv. 3,4).

The king described here, who defeated Xerxes, is Alexander the Great, whom we discussed in an earlier chapter. Once again, this prophecy was accurately fulfilled in history down to the last detail: At the height of his power Alexander's kingdom was "broken" and divided among his four generals. And the kingdom of Alexander did not fall to his descendants; they were assassinated. Thus Daniel's prophecy told about events of history that were still two hundred to four hundred years in the future.

The War Between the Kings of the South and the North

"Then the king of the South will grow strong, along with one of his princes who will gain ascendancy over him and obtain dominion; his domain will be a great dominion indeed" (v. 5).

As we have noted, two of the kingdoms resulting from the division of Alexander's empire attained prominence over the others: Egypt and Syria. The king of the South in this passage is Ptolemy Soter I, who ruled Egypt from 323 to 285 B.C. The king of the North was Seleucus Nicator I of Syria, who ruled from 312 to 281 B.C.

Seleucus Nicator was at one time driven out by Antigonus, who ruled Babylon. He sought refuge with Ptolemy Soter of Egypt. Aided by Egypt, he defeated Antigonus and became the king of Syria, ruling its vast territory stretching from Asia Minor to India. Thus he first received help from Egypt, but later his kingdom became stronger than Egypt, thereby opening the door to a war that lasted for the following 150 years.

> *"And after some years they will form an alliance, and the daughter of the king of the South will come to the king of the North to carry out a peaceful arrangement. But she will not retain her position of power, nor will he remain with his power, but she will be given up, along with those who brought her in, and the one who sired her, as well as he who supported her in those times"* (v. 6).

The details of this verse came true in later history. In order to cement diplomatic ties with the king of the North (that is, of Syria), Ptolemy II Philadelphus, king of the South (that is, of Egypt; 285-246 B.C.) wanted to marry his daughter Berenice to Antiochus II Theos of Syria (261-246 B.C.). Antiochus II had married before and already had a wife. But Ptolemy pressured Antiochus until he finally divorced his wife Laodice against his own will to take Berenice, princess of Egypt, as his new wife. But Antiochus could not forget his former wife, Laodice. So when his new father-in-law, Ptolemy, died of illness several years later, Antiochus brought Laodice back to the palace.

All this time Laodice had been waiting bitterly, watching for the opportunity to take revenge. So as soon as she was brought back to the palace, she murdered Antiochus, Berenice and their son, Antiochus III. Then she conspired to make her own son ascend to the throne of Syria so she could rule the kingdom through him.

Read verse 6 once again to see how precisely every detail was fulfilled. What an accurate prophecy this was—as it had to be, because it was given by God.

Syria and Egypt Continue to Fight

"But one of the descendants of her line will arise in his place, and he will come against their army and enter the fortress of the king of the North, and he will deal with them and display great strength. And also their gods with their metal images and their precious vessels of silver and gold he will take into captivity to Egypt, and he on his part will refrain from attacking the king of the North for some years. Then the latter will enter the realm of the king of the South, but will return to his own land" (vv. 7-9).

This verse is a prophecy of the things that would happen three hundred years after Daniel's time.

After Ptolemy II died, the brother of Berenice—the princess who had married Antiochus—ascended to the throne of the Egyptian kingdom. He became Ptolemy III Eurgetes (246-221 B.C.). Since he had waited for the opportunity to avenge the death of his sister, he finally raised a great army and made an expedition against Seleucus II Callinicus (246-226 B.C.) of Syria—the son of Laodice, his sister's murderer. But Syria was badly defeated by Egypt.

After this great war, acts of hostility ceased for several years as Syria regained strength. Then Syria raised a large army and made an expedition to Egypt in 240 B.C. But he was beaten again—exactly as the words of this verse had predicted.

"And his sons will mobilize and assemble a multitude of great forces; and one of them will keep on coming and overflow and pass through, that he may again wage war up to his very fortress" (v. 10).

When Seleucus II Callinicus of Syria thus failed in his expedition against Egypt, he fell sick and died of an illness. But his sons succeeded in the task. His first son, Seleucus III (226-223 B.C.), made several expeditions against Egypt, only to fail and die young. But he was followed by his younger brother, Antiochus III (223-187 B.C.), who defeated Egypt and took the Egyptian-held regions as far as the border of Gaza.

Note again that Daniel's prophecy concerning these sons actually took place three hundred years later. Phase after phase of this prophecy was fulfilled in history! Thus the Word of God is true, and not the smallest letter, not the least stroke of a pen, will fall to the ground.

"And the king of the South will be enraged and go forth and fight with the king of the North. Then the latter will raise a great multitude, but that multitude will be given into the hand of the former. When the multitude is carried away, his heart will be lifted up, and he will cause tens of thousands to fall; yet he will not prevail" (vv. 11,12).

Ptolemy Philopater (221-203 B.C.) of Egypt, who had lost his territories to Antiochus III, waged war against him in 217 B.C. with an army of seventy thousand. In the Battle of Laphia, near the border of Palestine, Ptolemy crushed Antiochus.

Antiochus not only lost his large army; he also had to hide himself in the desert, where he was almost taken captive. He narrowly escaped from death and fled—just as verse 11 had prophesied.

On the other hand, if the king of Egypt who had defeated Antiochus III at Laphia had gone on to Syria itself, sweeping everything in his way, he could have conquered the kingdom. But after he had slaughtered tens of thousands of enemy soldiers, he was filled with pride and ceased pursuing the enemy. Accordingly, after that time Egypt once again began to decline. This fact was prophesied in verse 12.

> *"For the king of the North will again raise a greater multitude than the former, and after an interval of some years he will press on with a great army and much equipment" (v. 13).*

Antiochus III, who narrowly escaped death in the desert, at last returned home. Bitter and seeking revenge, he prepared to make another expedition against Egypt. The long-sought opportunity finally came. Mysteriously, Ptolemy Philopater of Egypt and his wife died with no apparent cause in 203 B.C., and their only son, Ptolemy V Epiphanes, succeeded to the throne. But he was only a little child.

Seizing this opportunity, Syria invaded Egypt several times, like the flow of a tide. The prophecy recorded in verse 13 refers to this event.

> *"Now in those times many will rise up against the king of the South; the violent ones among your people will also lift themselves up in order to fulfill the vision, but they will fall down" (v. 14).*

At that time Israel was subject to Egypt, and the garrison of the Ptolemaic general Scopas was defending Jerusalem. Scopas showed much favor to the Jews, aiding them in refurbishing the temple and helping them in many other ways.

Nevertheless, when Syria invaded Egypt, many of the Jews stood with Syria against Egypt. Their plan was to take advantage of the conflict to drive Egypt from the country. But the plan ended in failure. Because of this behavior, Israel was branded a robber and an ungrateful nation. This event was prophesied in verse 14.

> *"Then the king of the North will come, cast up a siege mound, and capture a well-fortified city; and the forces of the South will not stand their ground, not even their choicest troops, for there will be no strength to make a stand" (v. 15).*

The Egyptian army of Scopas fought with the Syrian army in Farnia at the upper stream of the Jordan. But they were greatly defeated and had to retreat to the city of Sidon, which was known as the strongest fortress in the world at that time. Even so, the Syrian army attacked Sidon by building siege works all around the city, and the fortress finally fell between 199 and 198 B.C., and Scopas surrendered.

Thus Syria came to possess all the regions of Palestine and even Gaza at the border of Egypt, just as Daniel had prophesied. Elite Egyptian generals like Eropas, Manacles and Demonius tried hard to rescue Scopas when he was under siege. But they failed.

Rome Enters the Picture

> *"But he who comes against him will do as he pleases, and no one will be able to withstand him; he will also stay for a time in the Beautiful Land, with destruction in his hand. And he will set his face to come with the power of his whole kingdom, bringing with him a proposal of peace which he will put into effect; he will also give him the daughter of women to ruin it. But she will not take a stand for him or be on his side" (vv. 16,17).*

Then Syria, once it had crushed Egypt, brought to trial the Jews who had earlier rebelled against it, and Jerusalem once again came under the control of Antiochus III. Nevertheless, when Antiochus perceived the danger of Rome's advance east from Italy, he determined to make peace with Egypt, for he thought that further conflict with Egypt might threaten the security of his kingdom.

Accordingly, in order to carry out his plan, he gave his beautiful daughter, Cleopatra, to the seven-year-old King Ptolemy V Epiphanes of Egypt in marriage in 192 B.C. Her father hoped to gain control of the Egyptian throne through this marriage.

But Cleopatra sided with her husband, Ptolemy, against her father in several matters, so Antiochus's plan to make peace with Egypt failed. This situation was prophesied in detail in verse 17.

> *"Then he will turn his face to the coastlands and cap-ture many. But a commander will put a stop to his scorn against him; moreover, he will repay him for his scorn. So he will turn his face toward the fortresses of his own land, but he will stumble and fall and be found no more"* *(vv. 18,19).*

Eventually Antiochus gave up on Egypt and instead met with a Roman envoy who was traveling eastward at Lysimachus. The envoy proposed to Antiochus that he should surrender and pay tribute to Rome. But Antiochus answered proudly: "Asia has no interest in Rome, nor will she obey the command of Rome."

Having been thus insulted, Rome waited for the opportunity to take revenge on Antiochus. Meanwhile Antiochus, who up to that time had always succeeded in his expeditions to Egypt, made an expedition west into Europe, emulating Alexander the Great. His intention was to bring Greece under his control. But his European campaign ended in failure.

The Syrian advance was first checked at Turmophy, north of Athens, in 191 B.C. Two years later Syria was again badly defeated by an army led by the Roman consul Scipio at Magnesia, alongside the Maeander River southeast of Ephesus.

Antiochus III returned home disheartened from the failure of this campaign. Some time later he was murdered by an assassin while attempting to plunder a temple in the province of Elymais.

These historical facts also square with Daniel's prophecy in verses 18 and 19.

"Then in his place one will arise who will send an oppressor through the Jewel of his kingdom; yet within a few days he will be shattered, though neither in anger nor in battle" (v. 20).

After the death of Antiochus III, Seleucus IV Philopater succeeded to the throne. He surrendered to Rome and paid a tribute of several thousand talents every year. But when he had difficulty finding the fund for the tribute, he imposed heavy taxes on his own people and sent tax collectors to his tributary territories as well.

Seleucus sent a man named Heliodorus to be the tax collector for the Jewish nation. He was to seize the funds from the temple treasury in Jerusalem, but he died abruptly without any apparent cause. This is just what was predicted in verse 20.

Antiochus Epiphanes

"And in his place a despicable person will arise, on whom the honor of kingship has not been conferred, but

he will come in a time of tranquility and seize the kingdom by intrigue'' (v. 21).

The rest of the chapter following verse 21 is the key to the prophecy in the book of Daniel. The little horn which appears in 8:9-14, 23-25 of this book, namely Antiochus Epiphanes, arrives on the scene. He is a type of today's antichrist: He was a king who arose from Syria, and he devastated the temple of Israel.

In fact, he was a contemptible person who did not rightfully inherit the throne. When Seleucus IV Philopater died unexpectedly, he left two sons behind. The first son, Demetrius, was being held in Rome as a hostage. His second son, Seleucus, was still a young boy.

When their uncle Antiochus Epiphanes (175-164 B.C.) heard this news in Athens, he returned to Antioch under the pretext of becoming his nephew's regent. But after his return, he hired a man named Andronicus to kill his young nephew. Then he put Andronicus to death on a charge of treason, and he himself took the throne.

Consequently, his succession was not a rightful one but was accomplished by intrigue, as this prophecy had foretold.

"And the overflowing forces will be flooded away before him and shattered, and also the prince of the covenant" *(v. 22).*

Antiochus Epiphanes struck Egypt with a mighty army in 170 B.C. and crushed its forces in the region between Gaza and the Nile delta, which today is called Rasbaron. He also murdered Onias, the high priest of Israel, breaking the treaty of alliance he had made with him. This is the one referred to by Daniel as "the prince of the covenant."

"And after an alliance is made with him he will

*practice deception, and he will go up and gain power
with a small force of people" (v. 23).*

Thus Antiochus Epiphanes routed Egypt and ended the conflict with that nation. Then competition for the throne broke out in Egypt between his two nephews, the sons of Cleopatra. While Ptolemy Philometor and his young brother Ptolemy Euergetes were thus engaged in a fierce contest for the throne, Antiochus Epiphanes seized the opportunity to extend his power. He helped Ptolemy Philometor to become king—with the stipulation that Egypt would become subject to him in return. In this way Antiochus consolidated his power.

*"In a time of tranquility he will enter the richest parts
of the realm, and he will accomplish what his fathers
never did, nor his ancestors; he will distribute plunder,
booty, and possessions among them, and he will devise
his schemes against strongholds, but only for a time.
And he will stir up his strength and courage against the
king of the South with a large army; so the king of the
South will mobilize an extremely large and mighty army
for war; but he will not stand, for schemes will be de-
vised against him. And those who eat his choice food
will destroy him, and his army will overflow, but many
will fall down slain. As for both kings, their hearts will
be intent on evil, and they will speak lies to each other
at the same table; but it will not succeed, for the end
is still to come at the appointed time. Then he will return
to his land with much plunder; but his heart will be set
against the holy covenant, and he will take action and
then return to his own land" (vv. 24-28).*

After winning the hearts of his followers through the distribution of the spoil he had obtained from frequent pillages,

Antiochus Epiphanes mobilized an army and made another expedition to Egypt to attack his nephew. Egypt resisted strongly, but Syria made successive attacks.

During that time many treaties were agreed upon between the Egyptian king and the Syrian king. But even though they were close relatives (uncle and nephew), none of the treaties was kept, and they waged war against each other continually. Finally, Antiochus Epiphanes pounced on Egypt and seized much wealth from the country. Then, on his way back home, he also seized the treasures in the temple of Jerusalem.

"At the appointed time he will return and come into the South, but this last time it will not turn out the way it did before. For ships of Kittim will come against him; therefore he will be disheartened, and will return and become enraged at the holy covenant and take action; so he will come back and show regard for those who forsake the holy covenant. And forces from him will arise, desecrate the sanctuary fortress, and do away with the regular sacrifice. And they will set up the abomination of desolation. And by smooth words he will turn to godlessness those who act wickedly toward the covenant, but the people who know their God will display strength and take action. And those who have insight among the people will give understanding to the many; yet they will fall by sword and by flame, by captivity and by plunder, for many days. Now when they fall they will be granted a little help, and many will join with them in hypocrisy. And some of those who have insight will fall, in order to refine, purge, and make them pure, until the end time; because it is still to come at the appointed time" (vv. 29-35).

In 168 B.C., Antiochus Epiphanes again invaded Egypt, breaking their treaty. At that time, however, Egypt was under the regency of Rome.

Outside Alexandria, the Syrian king was confronted with the Roman envoy Gaius Popilius, who gave him a peremptory command. The envoy, who had already deployed his fleet in the Mediterranean, drew a circle where Antiochus Epiphanes stood and said, "Now choose before you come out of this circle, whether you will evacuate Egypt or attack her."

Epiphanes could not by any means resist the command of Rome. So he withdrew, full of anger. On his way home he stopped and took out his vengeance on Jerusalem. He destroyed the temple, violating the former covenant. He suspended the daily sacrifice. He set up an altar to Zeus Olympius, the pagan god he worshipped. And worst of all, he ordered a sow to be sacrificed under the abominable winged image.

Then the Jews arose in revolt under the leadership of Judas Maccabeus and his brothers. During the revolt, eighty thousand Jews were killed, forty thousand Jews were sold as slaves and another forty thousand Jews were carried off as captives. This was the greatest tragedy Israel had ever suffered from its involvement in the war between the kings of the South and the kings of the North. And it was all prophesied centuries before by Daniel.

Throughout this entire chapter of Daniel we can see how Daniel's prophecy was fulfilled in history down to the last detail. Yet some people do not believe that the book of Daniel was recorded two hundred to four hundred years before the incidents of the prophecy actually took place. Because they do not believe that prophecy is possible, they assert, "The book of Daniel is spurious, a fake prophecy which in reality was recorded after the things of the prophecy actually had happened. How otherwise could it be so accurate?'' But it is their own assumption that genuine prophecy cannot take place that causes them to be so foolish.

The King of the Last Time (11:36-39)

"Then the king will do as he pleases, and he will exalt and magnify himself above every god, and will speak monstrous things against the God of gods; and he will prosper until the indignation is finished, for that which is decreed will be done. And he will show no regard for the gods of his fathers or for the desire of women, nor will he show regard for any other god; for he will magnify himself above them all. But instead he will honor a god of fortresses, a god whom his fathers did not know; he will honor him with gold, silver, costly stones, and treasures. And he will take action against the strongest of fortresses with the help of a foreign god; he will give great honor to those who acknowledge him, and he will cause them to rule over the many, and will parcel out land for a price."

Antiochus Epiphanes, who produced this last series of tragedies, prefigures the antichrist who will arise in the last days, for the last antichrist will come and behave in the same way.

Up to verse 35 the prophecy was concerned with the war between the king of the South and the king of the North. But beginning with verse 36, the focus suddenly shifts to the antichrist who will appear at the end of time. As we have said, the two thousand years of the church age were hidden to the Jewish prophets.

In verse 36 we find a clear description of the antichrist who

161

will appear during the great tribulation. He will do as he pleases. He will exalt himself above all, claiming that he is divine. He will oppose the Lord God with unheard-of things. For seven years he will prosper. And that period will continue until the time of wrath is completed.

Thus Antiochus Epiphanes, who was dealt with in the passage up to verse 35, is immediately followed by a depiction of the antichrist, who imitates him.

The ensuing passage from verse 37 to verse 39 foretells how the antichrist will arise. It says that he will show no regard for the God of his fathers or for the desire of women, nor will he regard any god, but will exalt himself above them all. Here the God of his fathers refers to the Lord God of Israel. It was the dream of every Jewish woman that she might find favor from God and conceive the Messiah in her own womb. So Daniel is saying that the antichrist will have regard neither for God nor for his Messiah, Jesus Christ.

Here the details of the antichrist's background are more clearly revealed. The antichrist, like Antiochus Epiphanes, will come from Syria and will be a Jew. He will appear on the European political scene as a prominent politician, and he will accomplish the unification of ten European countries with his sternness and intrigue.

Daniel says that he will honor the god of forces, which means that he will worship Satan. The Bible shows that he will honor Satan with gold and silver, with precious stones and costly gifts. It also shows that he will build a strong fortress and conquer the whole world with the help of a foreign god—that is, through the strength of Satan. He will honor those who follow him, and he will distribute the land in return for a bribe.

The Last War of the Earth (11:40-45)

"And at the end time the king of the South will collide with him, and the king of the North will storm against him with chariots, with horsemen, and with many ships; and he will enter countries, overflow them, and pass through. He will also enter the Beautiful Land, and many countries will fall; but these will be rescued out of his hand: Edom, Moab and the foremost of the sons of Ammon. Then he will stretch out his hand against other countries, and the land of Egypt will not escape. But he will gain control over the hidden treasures of gold and silver, and over all the precious things of Egypt; and Libyans and Ethiopians will follow at his heels. But rumors from the East and from the North will disturb him, and he will go forth with great wrath to destroy and annihilate many" (vv. 40-44).

The prophecy following verse 40, combined with insights from the book of Revelation, shows that the antichrist will gain power while he rules over Europe for the first three and a half years, but he will also face rebellion in Africa when the tribulation passes into its second phase. When the rebellion arises in the confederate nations of Africa, centering in Egypt, the antichrist will make Jerusalem his headquarters for suppressing this uprising. He will make the temple of Jerusalem desolate and will set up his own image in it, destroying every Jew who does not bow down to it. Thus he will imitate Antiochus Epiphanes.

In this time of tribulation, however, the Jews will retire into a safe place prepared by God. This shelter is the city of Petra in Jordan, which was formerly the land of the Moabites and Ammonites. At this time God will bless the Jews by working a miracle, allowing them to flee away only one mile at a time.

163

For that reason, some British and American Christians are storing up at Petra a large quantity of canned food and Hebrew Bibles so that the Israelites may eat the food and read the Bible during the second three and a half years of tribulation. Petra is a shelter God has prepared for His people, a natural fortress impregnable to every attack by the enemy. Moreover, according to the prophecy, whenever the antichrist's army attempts to advance, the earth will open its mouth and devour it.

Consequently, the antichrist will have to turn his attention in the direction of Africa, especially Egypt. When he is about to strike Egypt, Libya and Ethiopia so that he can conquer and unify them, he will be alarmed by bad reports from the east and the north. The alarming news will be that the Euphrates River has dried up and a vast army of Asian people, led by China, is invading his country.

While advancing to the southwest, the army from the east will shower nuclear bombs. It will encounter the antichrist's army at the Valley of Jehoshaphat. This will be the Battle of Armageddon, which we have mentioned before. It will be a conflict on a scale unprecedented in human history.

"And he will pitch the tents of his royal pavilion between the seas and the beautiful Holy Mountain; yet he will come to his end, and no one will help him" (v. 45).

At the very moment when the antichrist destroys Israel and is engaged in the terrible war with the army from the east, placing his headquarters between the Mediterranean and the Dead Sea ("the seas") on Mount Zion ("the glorious holy mountain"), his end will come. Suddenly heaven will be opened, and Jesus will come down riding on a white horse. Countless numbers of redeemed people in white linen will follow him. By the sharp sword which comes out of his mouth, the Lord

Jesus will kill at once every person who has the mark of the beast. After overcoming the antichrist, the age of Jesus Christ and His saints will begin.

12

Israel and the End of History

The Great Tribulation (12:1)

"Now at that time Michael, the great prince who stands guard over the sons of your people, will arise. And there will be a time of distress such as never occurred since there was a nation until that time; and at that time your people, everyone who is found written in the book, will be rescued."

We have earlier discussed how the great seven-year tribulation is divided into two parts, each three and a half years long. When the second part of the tribulation comes to the Jews, Michael the archangel will arise and lead them to the fortress of Petra in Jordan. The antichrist will pursue them, setting in motion every weapon and piece of equipment he has.

If the Jews were to resort to running in that situation, it would not be long before they were all overtaken and put to death. But God will show them special favor through providing a way to escape. John says in Revelation:

And when the dragon saw that he was thrown down to the earth, he persecuted the woman who gave birth to the male child. And the two wings of the great eagle were given to the woman, in order that she might fly into the wilderness to her place, where she was nourished for a time and times and half a time, from the presence of the serpent (12:13,14).

Here the woman stands for the Jews. This prophecy shows that they will be enabled to flee swiftly to Petra. During this flight they will not be alone, but Michael the archangel will protect them. Those who escape to Petra will be the ones who are chosen among the Jews, and they will be those who love Jesus Christ.

The Resurrection (12:2-3)

"And many of those who sleep in the dust of the ground will awake, these to everlasting life, but the others to disgrace and everlasting contempt. And those who have insight will shine brightly like the brightness of the expanse of heaven, and those who lead the many to righteousness, like the stars forever and ever."

When Christ descends to this earth after the second three-and-a-half-year period is concluded, the great resurrection begins. Those who are beheaded during the seven years of the tribulation, especially the Jews, will arise to receive everlasting life. But remember that before the tribulation will have begun, those who rest in the earth will have risen first, with the voice of the archangel and the trumpet call of God, and after that those who are still alive will have been caught up together with them into the air to take part in the wedding of our Lord Jesus Christ. So those who rise at this point, at the end of the tribulation, are the martyrs who will be killed by the antichrist during the great tribulation.

Meanwhile, all the sinners who have opposed Christ will be killed by the sword which proceeds from His mouth, and they will be shut up in hell for a thousand years. Then the dead, great and small, will rise to stand trial before the great white throne. As soon as it is determined that their names are not recorded in the book of life, they will be thrown into the lake of fire burning with sulphur.

Then "those who have insight will shine brightly like the brightness of the expanse of heaven, and those who lead the many to righteousness, like the stars forever and ever" (12:3). "Those who have insight" refers to the people who wisely put off the lust of the flesh, the lust of the eyes and the pride of this world (see 1 John 2:16), and they are the people who wait for the coming of the Lord in constant watching and prayer.

Who then are they who will "lead the many to righteousness"? They are today's pastors, missionaries, home cell leaders, elders, senior deaconesses, deacons and ordinary Christians engaged in the propagation of the gospel of Jesus Christ to many people. These are the Christians who spend their time and energy to encourage the believers to cultivate a stronger faith while teaching the sinners who are ignorant of the truth the path of life to make them turn around. These people will shine forever, for they will shine with Christ.

When our Lord comes to this earth, He will reward us according to our labor. As the sun has one kind of splendor, the moon another and the stars another, and each star differs from another in splendor, so the reward God will give each of us will differ in glory (see 1 Cor. 15:40-42). So I pray in the name of our Lord Jesus Christ that you will preach the gospel to many people in order to receive a prize that will shine forever.

The End of the Revelation (12:4)

"But as for you, Daniel, conceal these words and seal up the book until the end of time; many will go back and forth, and knowledge will increase."

Daniel did not receive this revelation for his own sake or even for his own generation, but for us who live in the time of the end. He was told to close up and seal this revelation for us.

The book of Daniel was thus closed to the people who lived before us, so it was impossible for them to understand this book. By now, however, much of the revelation has passed into history, and Daniel is an open book to us. The time of the end is the very time when people go here and there swiftly, and knowledge increases. So the present time in which we come to possess the full knowledge of the Bible, by opening the seals from the Bible and by the increase of knowledge, is the very time when we are at the threshold of the end time.

The Final Period and Concluding Interpretation (12:5-13)

Then I, Daniel, looked and behold, two others were standing, one on this bank of the river, and the other on that bank of the river. And one said to the man dressed in linen, who was above the waters of the river, "How long will it be until the end of these wonders?" And I heard the man dressed in linen, who was above the waters of the river, as he raised his right hand and his left toward heaven, and swore by Him who lives forever that it would be for a time, times, and half a time; and as soon as they finish shattering the power of the holy people, all these events will be completed. As for me, I heard but could not understand; so I said, "My lord, what will be the outcome of these events?"

And he said, "Go your way, Daniel, for these words are concealed and sealed up until the end time. Many will be purged, purified and refined; but the wicked will act wickedly, and none of the wicked will understand, but those who have insight will understand" (vv. 5-10).

In his concluding vision Daniel hears a conversation about the end time. One man asks another: "How long will it be until the end of these wonders?" (v. 6).

The answer was given in words we have read before: "It shall be for a time, times, and half a time" (v. 7). This refers to the second period of three and a half years in the tribulation, during which the antichrist and his soldiers "finish shattering the power of the holy people," that is, the Jews (v. 7).

But Daniel could not understand these words, so he asked what would be the outcome of these events. But the only answer he received was to go his way, because the words were hidden and sealed until the end time.

But that is not the case for you. Happy are you who live at this closing time of the age of grace, because the words of Daniel are open to you.

In 1948 you may have witnessed Israel's rebirth as a nation after two thousand years of wandering.

Daily in your morning paper you read about the progress Europe is making toward unification.

You have succeeded in interpreting the secret of Daniel, and you are aware that when Europe is unified, from out of it will come a leader who is the antichrist foreshadowed by Antiochus Epiphanes. And you know that the great tribulation, the final week of Daniel, will begin as soon as he concludes a seven-year goodwill treaty with Israel.

Happy are you as well because you know that the people of God who believe in Jesus Christ will have been taken up into heaven by this time. You know that seven years after that the sanctuary of Israel will be destroyed and the power of the holy people will be broken. The people of God who have been taken up into heaven will come down to the Battle of Armageddon with Jesus Christ, who will take captive the antichrist and the false prophets. Though you will not be on this earth during the tribulation, you know quite well what will happen during this period.

Blessed are you who are among the wise at this time of the end. You understand the word of our Lord, and you are clean, for you have been washed by the precious blood of Jesus Christ. The foolish people will not be able to understand this secret which you know, even if they are given it in their hands and are taught about it.

Understanding the Different Numbers of Days

"And from the time that the regular sacrifice is abolished, and the abomination of desolation is set up, there will be 1,290 days" (v. 11).

This verse again confirms what will happen at the end of the world through the activity of the antichrist. But note here that the verse says, "And from the time that the regular sacrifice is abolished, and the abomination of desolation is set up, there will be 1,290 days." The period of three and a half years we have mentioned is equivalent to 1,260. Why are 30 days added here?

Here is the answer. Jesus will indeed come down 1,260 days after the abomination is set up, and that is exactly three and a half years. But before Jesus comes down, many people will have been killed in the Battle of Armageddon. In addition, when Jesus descends, He will destroy all His enemies who have gathered there with the sword that proceeds out of His mouth. So the number of people who will have been killed will roughly amount to three hundred million. Along with their bodies on the battlefield will be the weapons and the equipment they have left, which will be heaped as high as a mountain.

Once our Lord comes and casts the antichrist and the false prophets into the lake of fire, the battleground will have to be cleared of all the bodies and equipment. It will take thirty days for all these things to happen.

"How blessed is he who keeps waiting and attains to the 1,335 days! But as for you, go your way to the end; then you will enter into rest and rise again for your allotted portion at the end of the age" (vv. 12-13).

Then in verse 12, 45 days are added for a total of 1,335. The 45 days is the period needed for God to separate the sheep from the goats (see Matt. 25:31-46). Thus after His coming, for 30 days Jesus will put in order this world which has been destroyed. Then He will judge it in another 45 days. After that, the millennial kingdom will begin on this earth. It will take 1,335 days for all these things to be accomplished.

Are You Ready?

Even so, we will not need to wait until then. By this time we will have been taken up into heaven and will have descended with Jesus Christ when He comes down to put this world in order and to judge it. Afterward, we will reign with Him for a thousand years. When the period of this millennium is thus fulfilled, the new heaven and new earth, which are eternal, will wait for us.

Let me take the liberty of posing a few questions to you who have now finished reading this book:

DANIEL

Have you prepared the oil of the Holy Spirit in your life for the coming of the Bridegroom?

Are the members of your family all saved?

Have you brought your neighbors to the path of salvation?

We are just now passing over the threshold into the end time. The Lord is doing new things, and we must be ready.

OTHER BOOKS BY PAUL YONGGI CHO

The Holy Spirit, My Senior Partner
Understanding the Holy Spirit and His Gifts

Pastor Cho teaches in this book how we can learn about the person and work of the Holy Spirit, so that we can let Him guide us more effectively.   Trade paper $7.95

Praying With Jesus

In *Praying With Jesus* we learn what we should pray for and how we should pray for it. Cho also shows us that by praying more effectively we can learn to exercise our faith more boldly.
                                                       Hardback $10.95

Salvation, Health & Prosperity
Our Threefold Blessings in Christ

In 3 John 2 the heartfelt needs of every person are summed up and met by Jesus, who in Himself is the yes to all of God's promises to us.   Hardback $12.95

Available at your local Christian bookstore
or you may order from:

Creation House
190 N. Westmonte Drive
Altamonte Springs, FL 32714